The Mitford Society

Vol. III

Edited by Lyndsy Spence

www.facebook.com/themitfordsociety

www.themitfordsociety.wordpress.com

@mitfordsociety

❧ CONTENTS ❧

A FLY IN THE OINTMENT

A Mitford Tease

by

Lyndsy Spence & Meems Ellenberg

The echoing footsteps of Mabel along the long, narrow hallway of Rutland Gate caught Farve's attention. The sound of his Puccini aria spinning on the gramophone did nothing to dispel an impending sense of doom. As he watered his window box of fascinators – the seedlings he had scattered the year before – he made a mental note to check on Mr Dyer tending to the boiler in the basement. Being a fellow who was susceptible to the supernatural he pondered if Dyer, who lived a subterranean existence below the seven floors, was dead. It was a distinct possibility. Before leaving the library he locked his cold cup of coffee in the safe, lest some monkey's orphan should remove his suckments.

Farve passed Mabel, who held in her hand a lilac-coloured envelope. 'So gauche, so noveau-riche,' Muv had groaned when these bizarre envelopes had first started to appear on the tray of post. They were always addressed to Miss Nancy. 'What a stench!' Muv had choked, reacting to the overwhelming scent of tuberose. She knew with certainty, as she knew most things from her days on the high seas, that tuberose was responsible for many a debaucherous deed. 'Another one?' Farve approached Mabel, he was looking especially exotic in his paisley print dressing gown, sipping tea from a thermos and puffing on a gasper. He took the letter and examined it. A scattering of letters rudely cut from a magazine were glued to the lilac page. 'You are a charlaten and I hate you,' it read, though charlatan was spelled incorrectly. Having read only one book in his life, Farve failed to notice. 'I am a Mitford and I despise you,' the venom dripped off the page, or was it runny glue? 'You are ALL I despise,' it added once more in case the message wasn't clear.

'Who do you suppose it is?' Mabel asked. 'Not Jicksy, I should hope.'

Entering the drawing room, Farve asked the girls to gather around the fire. It was serious, Debo concluded, for they were allowed to abandon the jars of dripping jam on the sideboard and crumbs remained on the good table cloth.

'Such a bother,' Muv bemoaned. 'I should sooner send the table cloth up to Edinburgh than have beastly

Harrods charge me a king's ransom.'

No one remarked save Mabel, who may have been heard to mutter, 'Penny pinching peeress.'

Nancy, taking a break from preparing an article for *The Lady* magazine, slithered into the room. 'I say,' she rubbed the ink stains on her hands, 'I wish Snell would up my pay. This cheap ink is too, too sick-making.' Nobody spoke, presumably nobody cared. Nancy's constant complaints were what were too, too sick making, thought Decca, although her pique may have been due to another all-nighter reading Dorothy L. Sayers. So much bickering ensued about who said what to Mr Chatterbox about Diana's impending nuptials to Bryan Guinness, Pam's broken engagements and Nancy's fledgling literary career, that Farve had to bellow for silence. But, having to have the last word, Unity sneezed. 'Hatschie, Geräusch beim Niesen,' she said.

Delphine Ale-Stout, the letter was signed. Nancy and Diana wracked their brains but failed to place the name. 'Watney's Red Barrel,' Pam piped up and everybody laughed. She liked three-worded names: Purple-Sprouting-Broccoli, in particular.

'Perhaps we met her on the cultural cruise?' Debo suggested.

Unity and Decca wondered if Delphine Ale-Stout was a white slaver. 'It certainly sounds a white slaver name,' Decca mused.

'Sie sicherlich,' Unity agreed, something she seldom did.

'In English!' Muv exploded in a rare bout of bad temper. 'In English,' she said once more, repeating that, along with the King's English, she supported the Church of England, voted Conservative and believed in the afterlife – 'I should like to see Cecily,' she said. 'And Uncle Clem.' She spoke of the afterlife as though it were a meeting of the hounds, and certainly very English.

Ever since Nancy had started working for *The Lady*, Delphine Ale-Stout began to send her poison-pen letters. It all began rather incoherently, a jumble of letters and initials. 'HstCE,' one said in reference to that flippant tart Hamish St. Clair Erskine. 'NFM,' Nancy Freeman-Mitford retaliated. Though, as Blor pointed out, it could very well mean something else. 'Errr,' she scolded, 'no one will want to be your friend if that's how you talk.'

Then the letters spiralled out of control. Threatening words slipped through, warning that Delphine and her followers would kill her. Nancy vaguely remembered that one had the name of a colonial drink. 'It puts heaven in a rage,' Diana sighed.

Nancy was most vexed. Delphine Ale-Stout, a puzzle. Delphine Ale-Stout, a cipher. Delphine Ale-Stout, a rival writer. Delphine Ale-Stout, only a name in a sea of articles, never a fot. Delphine Ale-Stout: perhaps she did not have a photography face? Pathos personified. 'She eeees,' Nancy murmured.

'Oh blissipots!' Debo bubbled. Nancy's problems had been nothing to her as she had been invited by Uncle Matthew and Aunt Sadie to go shooting. Cousin Clementine wrote to say that Diana was welcome at Chartwell. Uncle Wolf wired an invitation to Fraulein Unity, but Muv said nein to 'going abroad with a stranger'. Decca, darling little D, was already packing for a weekend with the Paget twins. And, Pam, where was Pam? Surely she couldn't...Nancy snatched the letter. 'Charlaten,' her triangular green eyes honed in on the misspelling. Hmmm, poor Pam, she thought, always the thesaurus, never the dictionary.

'Here I am,' Pam breezed into the room in slow motion, her presence was as long and lingering as her vowels. 'I was just across town selling eggs to the Bed of Nails. Say!' she whipped two newspapers out of her basket, 'your tiff with Delphine Ale-Stout has made the front pages. Loooook!'

It was too sensational, too good to be true. 'Disney with knobs on!' Nancy squealed.

Blor, thinking a horrible accident had occurred, rushed into the drawing room. 'So sorry,' she gasped. 'I thought Miss Decca was on the roof again.'

'Look, Naunce,' Pam scanned the article. 'It says here that Delphine Ale-Stout has many occupations. She's a philanthropist. Haberdasher. And sometime chanteuse.'

'So non-U,' Nancy remarked.

Blor sniffed meaningfully.

The crossing to Dieppe was choppy. Decca opened her picnic hamper and noted Muv had packed a wholemeal loaf and Pam had boiled up a dozen new potatoes – a fitting luncheon for a farmer in a brown suit. The Paget twins agreed to meet her at the port, and together they would enjoy a motoring holiday around the Channel coast.

In the car, the twins rapidly spoke about a tour of Austria, and Decca listened intently to their itinerary. They would be staying with an elderly aunt, they said. 'A good alibi if one wanted to forge a naughty letter,' they added.

'I couldn't run away,' Decca's eyes widened at the thought. 'I haven't lodged my Christmas money for one thing. Besides, Cousin Winston would send a tanker to find me.'

'The mountains,' advised the Paget twins. 'No water to sail a tanker on in the mountains.'

They were brick girls, those Paget twins.

The following week another letter arrived for Nancy from Delphine Ale-Stout. This time she slipped up and included Lady as a prefix. Muv retrieved her well-thumbed copy of *Burke's Peerage* and scanned through the double-barrel names and the list of those tradesmen who had risen a rank or two. 'Really,' she was aghast; 'the peerage resembles a shopping-list these days.' There was no Delphine Ale-Stout, no Ale, no Stout...

Farve agreed, commenting that the peerage's pandering to household brands was lower than the belly of a snake. 'What next?' he harrumphed. 'Women in the House of Lords?'

'I don't see why not,' Pam looked up from polishing the silver. 'After all, you worked for a lady's magazine.' He scowled in reply and reminded himself that Pam's turn in Rat Week was long overdue.

'Settle down,' Muv scolded. 'After luncheon I shall read *Tess of the d'Urbervilles* aloud. Or would you prefer *White Fang*?'

They returned to the sick-making business of Delphine Ale-Stout. She had written a strongly worded, though incoherent, letter to rogue newspapers that dared to paint her as a villain. 'I committed no crime,' one of the more intelligible sentences read. She accused the newspapers of rewriting history and claimed that nobody would have heard of Miss Nancy Freeman-Mitford had she not put her on the map.

Nancy shrieked whether in joy or consternation, was unclear.

Farve's mind scrambled to his latest list of suspects. The Wid was swiftly added to it and, recalling the sight of a discarded handkerchief in a hedge, he included the Duchess of Marlborough. He also remembered that sewer with the comb in his breast-pocket. The list was growing.

But there was a twist at the end of this letter. Delphine Ale-Stout demanded a sum of money.

'Blackmail is such an unfortunate word,' said Muv.

Nancy could bear the riddle no longer. Delphine Ale-Stout demanded £50. She was explicit in her instructions. £50 in a lilac envelope (enclosed) should be left under an empty milk bottle at the Army and Navy stores on Victoria Street.

'The Army and Navy stores on Victoria Street?' repeated Farve. 'I shall escort you.'

Nancy and Pamela went along with Farve to the Army and Navy stores on Victoria Street. As Pam had errands to run on behalf of Muv, she left Nancy in a Lyon's teashop and told her to pay attention to the comings and goings at the stores. The morning rush was too divine and Nancy whipped out her pen and notepaper and began taking notes on the conversations on mantelpieces and settees ringing in her ears. She thought of constructing an article for *The Lady*, or perhaps a future book. Farve contented himself with reviewing the new shipment of entrenching tools.

Meanwhile in Dieppe, Decca had bumped into old Aunt Natty, otherwise known as Blanche Hozier, Farve's aunt. She was in high spirits, having come into an unexpected windfall of money. 'You must come to the casino,' she told Decca and the Paget twins. They agreed, whereupon they were introduced to Natty's admirer, the local and much-married fishmonger.

'How lucky to see you,' Natty said as she rolled the dice. 'We've just returned from our little benjo.' Pulling pound notes out of her handbag she ordered the fishmonger to place more bets.

'Where did you get all that money?' Decca enquired. The Paget twins were competing against one another at the billiards table.

'I pawned my Kodak,' said Natty.

'There must be fifty pounds in there,' Decca began to count the pound notes.

'Don't count, darling,' Natty snatched the money. 'Arithmetic is so unseemly for girls.'

'Oh look,' Muv drawled. 'Decca's written to say she bumped into Aunt Natty in Dieppe. 'She said Natty treated her and the Paget twins to a honnish evening in the casino and they went back to her house and gambled fifty pounds playing Snakes and Ladders.'

'Who won?' asked Nancy.

'Oh,' Muv rolled her eyes. 'She did not say.'

'Fifty pounds!' exclaimed Pam.

'Such a waste of money. Of course one can't help it if one's rich but....'

'Don't you see!' interrupted Pam. 'Don't you get it? Delphine Ale-Stout wanted fifty pounds. Naunce, you were at the teashop, tell them what you saw...'

'Well I...' Nancy thought for a moment. She decided to embellish the truth. 'I saw a very tall lady, very well-dressed with a Scottish terrier. She wore a cape over her nightgown, much to my everlasting embarrassment, you must understand.'

'Yes, and?' they shouted at once.

'Well that's all I saw,' she shrugged. 'So sorry.'

'Natty,' bellowed Farve.

'Natty,' whispered Muv.

'Telephone Cousin Winston,' he ordered his wife. 'We must send a tanker at once!'

Later that evening, Decca was back at Rutland Gate. The Paget twins caught a lift on the tanker and stopped off at Peter Jones to spend their Snakes and Ladders winnings. 'Five hours was all it took,' she chirped. Muv was most impressed at the efficiency. Pam said Dieppe was so close it was just like home. Nancy scoffed and said Paris was the place to be. Within the hour, Debo returned, covered in pheasant feathers and pigeons blood and weeping about a gruesome tale called *The Little Houseless Match*. Unity was upstairs, or so it was assumed by the goose-stepping thuds coming through the ceiling and the repeated playing of 'Horst Wessel Leid' on the gramophone.

'So tell me everything, from the start,' Muv ordered.

Decca said that Aunt Natty was her charming self and, after suggesting they go back to her house with the fishmonger, and having been hosed down at the front door, they all sat down to a thrilling game of Snakes and Ladders.

'Not Racing Demon?' Debo asked.

'No,' Decca stated. 'Oh, before I forget,' she reached into her pocket. 'Natty said to give you this.'

Narrowing her green eyes to slits, Nancy accepted the odoriferous lilac coloured envelope. 'Dare I open it?' She looked at Muv and Farve. Before awaiting their answer she tore into the envelope and realised there was fifty pounds inside.

'She is a good woman,' Muv said.

'Such a clever cove,' Farve agreed.

Like rich people, Muv told the children, some people could not help being naughty. Diana and Decca readily agreed and nodded in unison.

'Well, let's say we forget the whole ghastly business of Delphine Ale-Stout,' Nancy tossed the letter onto the fire.

'Whatever do you mean?' Decca jumped to her feet. 'Natty isn't Delphine Ale-Stout. She simply had no note-paper and the Paget twins came to the rescue.' With great difficulty she retrieved the half-singed letter from the fire. 'Money for an old war debt, love Natty,' she read aloud.

Blor sniffed. 'The Paget twins, eh?'

Five minutes later there was a knock on the door and Mabel entered, bearing another letter from Delphine Ale-Stout. It was an odd letter, quite rambling in its tone. 'Dearest Nancy Freeman-Mitford. I don't know who you are. I have never heard of you. I was impersonated by an old governess wishing to seek revenge and destroy my reputation. Please don't write back. I have blacklisted you.'

Nancy did not throw the letter onto the fire or tear it up. She added it to her pile of correspondence. 'One day I shall publish a book of letters, you'll see,' she told her disbelieving family.

They all laughed and forgot about the non-U escapade that was Miss Delphine Ale-Stout.

'One last thing,' Muv interrupted the jovial scene. 'What else did Natty say?'

'Oh,' Decca beamed, 'she promised to introduce me to her grandson, Esmond Romilly.'

There were *floods*. Absolute *floods*.

A BRIEF ENCOUNTER, A TERRIBLE FATE

Words by Lyndsy Spence

There was nothing exceptional about Diana's encounter with Adolf Hitler when she met him on 11 March 1935. Summoned by Unity, who succeeded in befriending the Fuhrer and worming her way into his inner-circle, Diana flew to Paris, collected the elegant Voisin which Oswald Mosley had bought for her, and motored to Germany. The events, before she met the Fuhrer, seemed far more memorable when she became stranded in heavy snow in the Black Forest, whereupon a passing peasant and his horses pulled her to safety.

Upon entering the Osteria Bavaria, Hitler's favourite restaurant in Munich, Diana discreetly remarked: 'Look at him [the Fuhrer] in his mackintosh.' From that low-key impression, she observed he 'appealed in equal measure to women and to exactly the sort of men he needed'. At the time, Diana could not speak German aside from a phrase or two, and she relied on Unity to translate. Although, on that particular day, there was more silence than conversation, and they stuck to polite small-talk. She claimed that she never heard Hitler rant, or go off on a political tangent.

However, the year before this meeting with Hitler, Diana had indeed witnessed his showmanship in person when she and Unity visited Munich on a whim because Putzi Hanfstaengl, a friend of her former in-laws, promised to introduce them to the Fuhrer. Having exaggerated his accessibility to Hitler, he produced two tickets to the Parteitag, and later refused them an introduction due to their heavily made-up faces. 'I can't do without my lipstick,' Unity said.

A year had passed since this false start. Unity had moved to Germany, and during a visit from Diana they looked up Hanfstaengle ahead of the second Parteitag, but he was less than accommodating and claimed to have no tickets. They went to Nuremberg and quickly discovered that the town was overrun by Nazis and their supporters, and, faced with the realisation there were no hotel rooms and no tickets, Unity spied an elderly man wearing a special badge. The badge in question indicated he was one of the Nazi Party's first members and, schooled on all things to do with Hitler, Unity approached him and confided their misfortune. He duly located a room and found two tickets. They went to the

Parteitag, now an elaborate militant display with special effects and blood-and-thunder music. Diana was lost in translation, but Hitler's passionate delivery and the crowd's enthusiasm inspired her to relay his mass appeal to Mosley, whose party was beginning to flounder.

In the near future when Diana learned German, she understood Hitler's message and it was clear to her, whether she believed it or not, just what he had planned for the Jews when he spoke of his Nuremberg Laws. She overlooked the rampant antisemitism of his speeches to focus on his aspirations for a great and powerful Germany, just like Mosley envisioned for Britain. She was, as her biographer Anne de Courcy wrote, very good at closing her eyes to anything she did not wish to see.

During the visit, Diana observed Hitler had simple tastes, apparent over luncheon at the Osteria Bavaria when he ordered 'eggs and mayonnaise, and vegetables and pasta, and compote of fruit or a raw grated apple, and Fachingerwasser'. She was further impressed by his European manners: he kissed her hand, bowed his head and did not sit down until she was seated. This, she felt necessary to mention in her autobiography, *A Life of Contrasts*, given the 'acres of print about Hitler in which his rudeness and bad manners to everyone are emphasised'. Hitler fascinated her with his grey-blue eyes, so dark that they often appeared brown and opaque. And like many who possess sinister intentions, he charmed her.

The charm was in abundance; he admired Unity and Diana, the latter in her chic Parisian clothes. And, unlike many in his company, the sisters were not intimidated by him and they conversed freely, often punctuating their sentences with Mitford jokes and witty nuances. To dispel the myth surrounding Unity's head-over-heels infatuation with Hitler, Diana wrote: 'Unity was never awed in her entire life. She said what came into her head.' It was this candour which made the Fuhrer laugh and, in return, 'he inspired affection'.

After their short stay in Munich, Diana and Unity went to Paris, each taking turns to drive the Voisin. Paris never appealed to Unity the way it did to Diana, and after exhausting the museums and galleries, she left for Germany.

That brief meeting, eight decades ago, marked a watershed moment in Diana's life and the decisions that would ultimately seal her fate. Unity, the channel to Hitler, spoke glowingly of Mosley and his British Union of Fascists. When she reported that Hitler showed an interest in meeting Mosley, Diana jumped at the opportunity to form an alliance between the two men.

It does not take a genius or a well-versed Mitfordian to predict what happened next.

ABSCHIEDE

Words by Meems Ellenberg

She opened her eyes slowly and willed herself awake. She loved opening her eyes each morning in the bedroom in her new pretty flat. She had decorated it in so much excitement, and everything she saw made her happy. The flags draped over her headboard, the light streaming through the windows, and especially his picture on her nightstand. 'Today is the day,' she thought and shivered.

The call came fairly early, so there was no time for coffee or breakfast. She hurried into the small bathroom to wash and make up. She dressed with particular care, and gently brushed her blonde hair, so as not to disturb the hairdresser's careful set. She wished there was time to visit again today, but no matter. It really didn't matter.

The weather was warm for September, so she decided against a coat. Just the jacket of her suit would be enough. She would be driving to and from her errands, darting in and out of the car, until just the last one.

The putzfrau wouldn't be in, so she locked the door and raced down the stairs. She felt a queer and giddy excitement bubble up inside her, and she found her mouth continually stretching to a grin.

She was not terribly worried about what the telegram at the Consulate would say, as she really already knew. It was so sad, of course, and so unnecessary, but she knew what she had to do and she was ready. She wasn't afraid. Nervous, perhaps, like before a dance, or nervous like the first time she saw him, from a distance. Or the first time she met him, trembling like a leaf. But not afraid. Because it was for him.

She walked from the Agnesstrasse to the Consulate. She asked at the desk, and the clerk handed her the telegram. The news was as she had expected: war had been declared.

She asked for pen and paper, and quickly wrote a note back to her parents. She asked the clerk to take it back to England. She thanked him, and taking a deep breath, headed for the Gauleiter's headquarters at the Interior Ministry.

She asked to see him, and was shown into his office. She liked Gauleiter Wagner, and trusted him. She quietly asked if she was to be interned as an enemy alien. He was calm and reassuring and told her that would certainly not be the case. He asked how she was set for petrol for the car. No, no, no petrol, thank you, but she felt her anxiety rising. She asked him to promise that no matter what happened, she would remain in Munich. He said of course she would remain in Munich.

The walk back to the flat was a blur. She saw nothing. She heard nothing. Everything had come down to this day. She thought only of all the things she had to accomplish, mentally ticking off the list.

She let herself in, and allowed herself a fond look at the colourful furniture, the flowers, and the big pile carpet. How she loved the little flat, with its sitting room, comfortable drawing room, the bedroom, and the balcony. How lucky the previous owners had decided to go abroad. She decided to telephone Rudi.

Rudi, of course, was no help at all. She begged her not to do anything, but to go to Burgenland until tomorrow. All she could say was, 'No,' and a quick goodbye, and she abruptly placed the receiver back into the cradle. No, she would not take Rudi's advice. This was no time to get away until 'things died down', as Rudi thought. The time was now, and she had to do it. She had said so. She had said so to Rudi, to Diana, to the Schaubs, to everyone.

There was no turning back.

She gathered up the things she would need. She let herself out again, listening for the quick click of the lock. She opened the door to her car and settled behind the wheel. She started up the ignition, thrilled, as always, as the powerful machine hummed to life. The car had been his gift, and was so like him: so new and exciting and sleek and powerful. He had been so good to her. And she would finally repay his goodness.

She drove rapidly — as she always did, with little use for turn signals or mirrors or pedestrians. She arrived in no time at the main shopping district and quickly parked.

She stopped in at a few shops, settled some small bills with the shopkeepers, and then stopped in at her singing teacher's flat. Raventos was not in, but she visited briefly with Nina, and gave her an envelope with her keys in it, and asked that it be delivered to Rudi tomorrow. Nina agreed, and she left, again, in a hurry.

She drove back to Wagner's office. Abruptly clicking off the ignition, she collected the envelope from the seat beside her. She strode in, gaining confidence and resolve, and asked again to see the Gauleiter. She handed him the large envelope, and cautioned him as he took it from her that it was heavy. He laughed and said indeed it was. She watched him place it atop the piles of papers and telegrams and dispatches, and stood for a moment, before saying goodbye and ducking back into the car.

She steadied herself for a moment behind the wheel, mentally checking that she had taken care of everything and then satisfied she had – save for the one final thing, the most important thing – drove off.

It was time to do it.

She had thought about this and she knew the perfect place. It was close to her flat on the Agnesstrasse, and she had often walked the dogs there. She smiled as she remembered her secret escapade of nude sunbathing in a secluded spot, convulsed with giggles of what her mother would have thought. Yes, the Englischer Garten was perfect.

She parked the car and switched it off. She picked up her purse and got out of the car. She walked to the park on Koniginstrasse, towards the art museum. She found a bench and sat for a moment to reflect.

It was a beautiful day in the city she loved so much. Her dreams had all come true here. She had met him. They had become friends, good friends: laughing and lunching and taking tea and sharing jokes. He had talked to her as he talked to no one else of his vision for the future, his plans for Germany, his plans for the world. He was the greatest man in the world, and she would give him what she had said she would.

She opened her bag and took out the small silver pistol with the pearl handle. Her hand did not shake. She fired one shot into the ground.

Then she raised the pistol to her temple and fired again.

Meems Ellenberg is a former actress, waitress, nanny, fundraising executive, and hotel manager. She lives on the North Coast of the Dominican Republic and is the mother of a red-headed son. She is a proud member of The Mitford Society.

MUV IN WONDERLAND

Words by Kathy Hillwig

Everyone knows of the Mitford girls – and the Mitford girls knew everyone. There were few celebrities of the early 20th century that at least one of the Mitfords had not met. One is less inclined to think of Sydney Redesdale (née Bowles) in those terms, yet she also knew an assortment of the famous and colourful people of the time, including Lewis Carroll, the nom de plume of Charles Dodgson.

This year is the 150th anniversary of the publication of *Alice's Adventures in Wonderland*. Sydney Bowles was not born when the book was published, in 1865, but her father, Thomas Bowles, was a friend of Charles Dodgson. Remaining in touch with Dodgson, he naturally took an interest in his friend's offspring.

In May 1891, when Sydney was 11-years-old, Dodgson sent her a letter, and enclosed was a copy of *Alice's Adventures Underground*. Perhaps, given that her birthday was in May, it was a birthday present from the author. From the tone of the letter, it is evident that Sydney had not met Dodgson, for he writes that he 'didn't know of your <u>existence</u>' before 'hear[ing] that you had sent me your love!'

Formerly a mathematics tutor at Cambridge before finding fame as a novelist, Dodgson had a predilection for young girls. He met Mary Prickett and was introduced to her three charges, the Liddell girls: Ina, Alice (the inspiration for his novel) and Edith, and he visited the family home and photographed the girls without their mother's consent. He would go on to take nude photographs of the then 14-year-old Ina – this was not uncommon in the Victorian era. It was also fairly common in the Victorian era for an adult male to take a fancy or become engaged to a female child (perhaps in her teens) and wait until she was of age to marry. However, his fixation with the 11-year-old Alice was a daring one, even in those days. A book, *The Looking Glass House*, based on the Liddells, Dodgson and their governess Mary Prickett, who loved him and saw her charges as her rivals in love, was written by Alice Liddell's granddaughter, Vanessa Tait. On the subject of letters to his 'child friends', it should be noted that Dodgson's love-letters to Alice were discovered by her mother, hidden in her dollhouse. His visits and association with the family came to an abrupt end.

Back to his correspondence with Sydney, the letter is fairly unsettling by today's standards. He writes: 'If only I had known you were existing, I would have sent you <u>heaps</u> of love, long ago. And, now I come to think about it, I ought to have sent you the love, without being so particular about whether you existed or not.' Perhaps, a lonely man himself, he felt an infinity with Sydney, a young, motherless girl, who spent her childhood on her eccentric father's yacht, sailing the Mediterranean and the Orient. Whatever the nature of his feelings and the truth behind his motive for befriending Sydney, it amounted to nothing.

The letter is dated May 22 1891, and is reproduced in Sophia Murphy's book, *The Mitford Family Album*. On the facing page is a picture of an 8-year-old Sydney Bowles, looking very much like Dodgson's romantic vision of Alice. The letter and book – which Dodgson notes is 'the book just as I first wrote it, with my own pictures' – seem just another example of the Mitford way of being, quite effortlessly, in the thick of every interesting event.

❦ Kathy Hillwig lives in eastern Kentucky. Her dream holiday would be a week at Chatsworth, drinking tea and binge-reading the sisters' correspondence.

EVELYN WAUGH AND HIS CIRCLE

Words by Jeffrey Manley

A conference was organised by the University of Leicester earlier this year on Evelyn Waugh and His Circle: Reading and Editing the Complete Works. The conferees included three keynote speakers as well as 80 delegates, 29 of whom offered papers. Since the Mitfords were very much part of Waugh's 'circle', it is not surprising that they made multiple appearances.

The most important Mitford-related presentation was that offered by the first keynote speaker, (Lady) Selina Hastings. She has written biographies of both Nancy Mitford (1985) and Evelyn Waugh (1995). In introducing her, Alexander Waugh, the novelist's grandson, remarked that her Waugh biography (one of four full length versions) was unique in that she had personally interviewed such a wide assortment of Waugh's friends and acquaintances shortly before their deaths. Her talk was titled 'Evelyn Waugh and Nancy Mitford: A Literary Correspondence Course'. This focused on the period from 1945 to 1960 during which Waugh sought to act as mentor to Nancy in the production of her final four novels.

The two writers had known each other since the late 1920s when Nancy had been the flatmate of the woman who became Evelyn's first wife. After his messy divorce, Nancy sided with Evelyn. They became closer friends during the war when they saw each other frequently at the Heywood Hill bookstore that was next door to Waugh's barber in Mayfair. Nancy provided Waugh with information, books and gossip while he was secluded in Devon writing *Brideshead Revisited* and later in Yugoslavia on military duty.

Hastings quotes extensively from their letters to provide an insight into how Waugh tried to influence her writing. But she also points out how he himself picked up useful information from her. He sent her an advance copy of *Brideshead Revisited* and was anxious for her comments. She gave him valuable advice, for example, pointing out his mistaken reference to a piece of jewellery, which he corrected in later editions. She also imparted gossipy information on the reactions of his friends to the novel. She explained that she, too, had started a new novel to be about her family but needed time off from the bookstore to concentrate on it.

She received three months leave in early 1945 to write her book. She wrote at her sister Deborah's house in Derbyshire and the words came compulsively and easily, something that never happened again. Hastings says this may have had to do with her state of mind as she was deeply in love for the first time (with Gaston Palewski) and had found a new maturity. Waugh helped her select a title, rejecting her original proposal of *Linda*. When he read the manuscript, he declared the first half to be good, but he thought that the second half needed to be rewritten. He told Diana Cooper that Nancy had written half a good novel. When Nancy said she hadn't time for an extensive rewrite, he told her it would be worth the effort even if the improved version wouldn't appear until the Penguin edition. But she demurred, deeming it the best she could do.

Hastings dates from this point what she describes as a teacher/pupil relationship between Waugh and Nancy. *The Pursuit of Love* appeared in December 1945 and Hastings says it was the perfect timing for such a book – funny, frivolous and sweepingly romantic; the perfect antidote to the long war years. It was very successful and with the royalties Nancy was able to move to Paris where she could be nearer to Palewski. Once she had settled, she told Waugh she wanted to start a new novel but couldn't get a plot in mind. He told her she had used up too much of her best material in the first novel but warned her to keep the story in England where she knew the place and people intimately. He also warned her against any 'Britain can take it' novel about the camaraderie at the warden's post.

She finally came up with a story in September 1947 based on a family she barely knew. This became the Montdores. Waugh agreed that she could write in the first person again, using Linda as her narrator. But she had to make up most of the story and build the characters, so this was a much slower process than *Pursuit*. She didn't have a manuscript until a year later. Waugh said it was a good story but not yet a book. It needed 6-months of hard work. He provided detailed comments on what she needed to do but, again, the teacher was too ambitious for his student. *Love in a Cold Climate* was published in July 1949 to even more positive acclaim than *Pursuit*.

Notwithstanding Nancy's rejection of most of his advice, Hastings notes that there is ample evidence of how her writing was influenced by his. For example, she used some of the same or related real life characters that he had used as models. Her mother-in-law, Lady Rodd, became the model for Lady Montdore. Waugh used Alistair Graham's mother (Jesse Graham) as the model for Lady Circumference. The two character models were related by marriage and shared many traits. Peter Rodd himself inspired much of Basil Seal's character as he did those of both Linda's husbands, Tony Kroesig and Christian Talbot. Cyril Connolly was the model for both Waugh's Everard Spruce and Nancy's Ed Spain, and Diana Cooper was the basis for both Julia Stitch and Lady Leone.

When Nancy wrote the next novel in this series, *The Blessing*, Waugh once again offered extensive and detailed comments. This time, he included suggestions relating to her grammar and usage and sent her a copy of Fowler. As before, she ignored most of his advice. He nevertheless declared the book a success, even though Hastings describes its critical reception as less enthusiastic than was the case for the first two. After this experience, he largely gave up his tutorial role. Nancy's last novel, *Don't Tell Alfred*, was not at all well received by the critics. Although Waugh was upbeat in his own assessment, he offered no proposals for improvement. After this, Nancy wrote no further novels, instead concentrating on historical biographies.

Waugh tried to make light of her rejection of his advice, reckoning that only about 1,000 readers were likely to appreciate the improvements he proposed, and even those readers would enjoy the satisfaction of reading the unrevised text and themselves catching the author out. He also counseled against republication of the pre-war novels unless they were substantially revised. And when she asked how he dealt with letters from readers, he gave her several different categories that merited differing treatments.

After Hastings's talk, there was a 20 minute Q&A session in which other Mitfords were mentioned: Diana, Tom and Unity. The highlight of that session was Hastings's description of the meeting she arranged between Diana Mitford and A.N. Wilson, although a close second would be her equally hilarious description of her interviews with Gaston Palewski. Also not to be missed is her imitation of Diana's 'Mitfordspeak' accent, in both English and French.

Another talk, unrelated to the Mitfords, raised an interesting point on which Hastings had commented. Mary Frances Coady gave a paper entitled 'Enthralling Task: Evelyn Waugh Edits Thomas Merton.' This is based on her recent book *Merton & Waugh: A Monk, A Crusty Old Man, and the 'Seven Story Mountain'*. She describes Waugh's attempts to improve the prose style of best-selling Roman Catholic cleric, Thomas Merton – an American. In this case the task began with Waugh's editing for the U.K. publication of Merton's first book, *Seven Story Mountain*. He removed what he considered 'redundancies and solecisms', shortening it by about 80 pages and retitling the revised version, *Elected Silence*. A series of letters followed, much like those between Waugh and Nancy, in which Waugh tried to offer Merton advice for improving his writing. He also sent Merton a copy of Fowler. But Merton, although appreciative of Waugh's efforts, continued to write in what Waugh considered an unnecessarily repetitive manner. In the final analysis, the public seems not to have been troubled by Merton's inferior (in Waugh's opinion) writing style. *Elected Silence* fell out of print while *Seven Story Mountain* is still being published.

Another keynote address, 'Partial Lives, Obscure Lives', mentioned several Mitfords. This was by Paula Byrne, author of the biographical study or 'partial life' *Mad World: Evelyn Waugh and the Secrets of Brideshead* (2010). Her talk related the story of Kathleen ('Kick') Kennedy, the sister of JFK and a devout Roman Catholic, and her wartime marriage to William Cavendish, Marquess of Hartington, heir to the Devonshire title and estates, and an equally devout Anglican. This is the subject of Byrne's latest book that is to be published in early 2016. Waugh had first met Kathleen at a dinner party in 1938 and considered her a friend but advised her against the marriage on religious grounds.

At the beginning of the talk, Byrne mentions the three woman friends that Waugh 'worshipped' to the end of his life.

Two of these were Mary Lygon, and Waugh's second wife, Laura. The third was Diana Mitford. She describes Waugh's devotion to Diana in 1929 and how they drew apart after the birth of her first child, Jonathan Guinness. Following that, he moved on to the Lygon sisters. Byrne also mentions how Diana and Waugh became reconciled in the months before Waugh's death in 1966 when they began to communicate.

Briefly mentioned was Deborah Mitford. After the death of Kathleen Kennedy's husband, his brother Andrew (Deborah's husband), inherited his title and became heir apparent to the dukedom and estates. In the Q&A following the talk, Byrne explains how Deborah befriended Kathleen following her husband's death and how the Cavendish family allowed her the use of their Lismore estate in Ireland for entertaining visiting friends and family. Byrne also displayed a photo of Kathleen's gravestone at Chatsworth, which later became a place of pilgrimage for members of the Kennedy family. She doesn't mention in the talk (but may well do so in the book) how Deborah had become closely acquainted with Kathleen during their 1938 debutante season in London. Nor does she describe how Deborah and her husband became close to the family of JFK during his presidency, attending, *inter alia*, both his inauguration and funeral. She does mention, however, how Kathleen as a debutante charmed the British establishment and press corps with her relaxed American ways, including her reference to the 10th Duke of Devonshire (soon to be her father-in-law) as 'Dooky Wooky'.

In my paper, relating to edits Waugh made to the final volume (*Unconditional Surrender*) of his war trilogy, Nancy Mitford is mentioned for having inadvertently contributed to one of the changes ('Guy's Deleted Nippers: The Unending Saga of the Ending to *Unconditional Surrender*'). Having received an advance copy, she wrote Waugh on 22 October 1961 to say 'how glad I am about the happy ending'. In an epilogue to the story, Waugh had written that the hero Guy Crouchback had remarried after the war and that he had two children with the new wife. These were in addition to the child that he had legitimised by remarrying his first wife after he learned she was pregnant from an extramarital affair. Nancy went on to opine that 'I expect they will like Trimmer's kid [the legitimised child] far better than their own'. Waugh responded tersely to Nancy's praise for the ending that 'only Box-Bender thought the ending happy'. He was referring to Guy's dense, middle-class, Protestant brother-in-law who was rather clueless about family matters and things in general.

Based on Nancy's letter and a contemporaneous comment from novelist Anthony Powell, who thought the 'happy ending' unsuccessful, Waugh decided to change the ending, even though the book had already been published. He explained to Powell:

> I am disconcerted that I have given the impression of a 'happy ending.' This was far from my intention. The mistake was allowing Guy legitimate offspring. They shall be deleted from any subsequent edition. I thought it more ironical that there should be real heirs of the Blessed Gervase Crouchback dispossessed by Trimmer but I plainly failed to make that clear. So no nippers for Guy and Domenica in Penguin. (*Letters of Evelyn Waugh*, p. 579)

The paper goes on to describe how the belated change never appeared in the Penguin edition, and how subsequent editions, translations, and dramatic adaptations of the book are inconsistent as to which ending they reflect.

Nancy Mitford was also briefly mentioned by other speakers. In a paper by Rebecca Moore on 'Darling Dandies: The Female Dandy in Waugh's Interwar Novels', Nancy Mitford's description of a female dandy is cited. This is her reference to Waugh's first wife as 'looking like a ravishing boy, a page'. In the Q&A that followed, a member of the audience made the comment that Waugh's character, Julia Stitch, who Moore had identified as a female dandy, was like a Mitford character in that she survived by reliance on a performance exemplifying flightiness or excessive femininity. The other female dandy characters cited by Moore were Agatha Runcible and Mrs. Rafferty. In a paper offered by Michael Shawcross ('Going to the Devil: Evelyn Waugh, Kingsley Amis and the Self-implicating Decline Narrative') correspondence between Waugh and Nancy is cited to illustrate their mutually negative views of Amis. There were a few references to this correspondence by other speakers, but these quoted only Waugh's letters, rather than Nancy's.

☙ Jeffrey Manley is a retired lawyer who lives in Austin, Texas, not far from the Harry Ransom Center that is home to the archives of Evelyn Waugh, among many others. He is an active member of the Evelyn Waugh Society and contributes to their journal and conferences. He is also active in the Anthony Powell Society of which he is a trustee.

WHY DOES THE BRITAIN OF THE EARLY 1900S INTRIGUE AND DELIGHT SO MANY OF US?

Words by Tessa Arlen

Today the great houses of Britain's landed aristocracy with their vast, exquisite and often drafty interiors and views of sweeping parkland attest to the power of rank and wealth of a bygone age. They also provide a stunning backdrop for elegantly clothed men and women with gracious manners who star in numerous costume dramas. We are presently enraptured by the first two decades of the 1900s.

Let us ignore for the moment those gracious country houses that have survived to continue to provide their families with shelter, by providing the public with a place to picnic, or watch a steam engine rally, or drive through a safari park. It is a spectacularly golden July day and you have been invited for a Saturday-to-Monday, as the Edwardians called a weekend, to one of their glorious country houses. Here is a little advice to bear in mind for your short stay, after all you might want to be invited back!

Whatever you do don't alienate the servants. It is important not to underestimate how the Edwardians related to those who ensured their comfort and provided them with flawless and devoted service. Servants employed in the great houses were part of the family, but not of it; a sizable distinction because it relies on generations of subtle understanding of the polite, but offhand tact, used by the uppers when they addressed the lower orders. Butlers, footmen and personal maids will be extraordinarily unforgiving if you wear incorrect attire for the country, and cruelly punishing if you are either patronisingly familiar or arrogantly dismissive. So beware! The butler and the housekeeper will be far more intimidating than the charmingly eccentric dowager duchess or that affable old colonel you will be seated next to when you arrive in time for tea.

Your Edwardian great-grandmother would have been able to give you some good advice. Huge pointers for your comportment this weekend would be restraint, restraint, and more restraint in a way we can't begin to imagine today.

Your great-grandmother would be the first to remind you to lower your voice to a well-modulated murmur, that it is rude to interrupt, or even be too enthusiastic. Do not comment on your surroundings, the magnificence of the house, or marvel at the deliciousness of your dinner. You are not on a 'girls' night out', no matter how confiding and wickedly risqué your new Edwardian girlfriends appear to be, or how many glasses of wine the footman pours for you at dinner. So sorry, I meant to say self-restraint – just place your hand, palm down, over your wine glass to indicate no thank you, when you feel a delighted shriek start to emerge.

This was a time when women were treated like goddesses . . . then they married and were kept at home to incubate an heir and a spare. While the men at your country house weekend might enjoy shooting and fishing, you are encouraged to watch and applaud, but not join to in. By all means pick up that croquet mallet if that is your sort of thing, and certainly a game of lawn tennis is permitted, if you can actually move in your pretty afternoon dress and that killing corset. When the gentlemen sit back to their port and a cigar after dinner your hostess will beckon you away with the other women – important that you go with them. Despite the luxurious existence of the early 1900s, most women today would find it impossible to live the hidebound, restricted life of early 20th century women. So after you have lugged in the groceries after a hard day at the office, made dinner and then helped the kids with their homework before putting them to bed, just in time to collapse on the sofa to catch an episode of *Downton*, try not to sigh too deeply when Mathew Crawley goes down on one knee in the swirling snow to propose to Lady Mary. Most of us would have been Daisy slogging away in the scullery and not Lady Grantham reading a novel in the drawing room.

Did the Edwardian Shangri-La portrayed in *Downton Abbey* ever really exist even for the upper-classes? The short answer is 'yes' if you were Lord Grantham and not his servant, his wife or any of his daughters. If you have a problem not seeking to right the inequities of life, then don't get on that train at London's Marylebone station for the country. Certainly there were drunken, abusive husbands, negligent and thoughtless parents, spendthrifts and philanderers in the Edwardian age . . . and wronged wives looked the other way. The trick to coping with the darker side of human nature, if you were of society, was that it must never be referred to, never confided and most definitely never publicly acknowledged. However if you are an egalitarian at heart and social ostracism doesn't bother you too much, you might join Mrs Pankhurst's suffragettes and loudly proclaim your opinions. I have heard that Holloway Prison was equipped with a special wing for militant members of the WSPU.

The third housemaid will unpack your trunk for you – five changes of clothes a day for three days need an awful lot of tissue paper. Here's a titillating scrap of fresh society gossip to share with the company – gossip was the spice of Edwardian life – a substitute for reality TV. Gladys, the Marchioness of Ripon, an ultra-sophisticate with a 'past' was a wonderful example of the Edwardian double-standard and loved to gossip with her close coterie of friends. Alone in her lover's house one day she discovered a pile of rivetingly indiscrete love letters written to him by one of her social adversaries, Lady Londonderry. Gladys swiped the lot and generously shared the juicy bits – read aloud after dinner – to her closest friends. After the fun was over she honorably returned the letters to their author at Londonderry House – when she knew husband and wife were dining alone. The butler approached his lordship and handed over the ribbon-bound bundle. After studying the contents, in silence, Lord Londonderry directed his butler to carry the letters to the other end of the dining table. Silence still reigned as Lady Londonderry came to terms with her awful predicament, a silence that was never broken between the two of them again. Far worse than having an affair, Lady Londonderry had 'let down the side'. Adultery was a fact of life, indiscretion unforgivable; to be the subject of common gossip shameful and the scandal of divorce out of the question. Lord Londonderry never spoke to his wife in private again, and maintained a distant, cold courtesy to her in public for the rest of their long marriage.

So much more entertaining than a splashy tabloid divorce, don't you think?

🐝 Tessa Arlen, the daughter of a British diplomat, had lived in or visited her parents in Singapore, Cairo, Berlin, the Persian Gulf, Beijing, Delhi and Warsaw by the time she was 16. She went to the U.S. in 1980 and worked as an H.R. recruiter for the Los Angeles Olympic Organizing Committee for the 1984 Olympic Games, where she interviewed her future husband for a job. She is the author of the Lady Montfort mystery series. And lives on an island in the Puget Sound, Washington.

THE CIVILIAN BOMB DISPOSING EARL, COUSIN CIMMIE AND OSWALD MOSLEY

Word by Kerin Freeman

I am the author of *The Civilian Bomb Disposing Earl* (Pen & Sword, 2015) which explores the life of Jack Howard, the 20th Earl of Suffolk & Berkshire. Born in 1906 in Wiltshire, England, to Henry Molyneux Page Howard, the 19th Earl of Suffolk and Berkshire, and the American heiress, Marguerite Hyde (née Leiter), known as Daisy. The worlds of the aristocracy and the American heiress were an hedonistic combination, and Daisy made quite an impression on society. She cut a striking figure at 6-feet-tall, and as the daughter of a former impoverished clerk who later became a millionaire, Daisy was the epitome of nouveau-riche.

Daisy was the middle-child of three daughters, Mary the oldest and Nancy the youngest, there was also a son, Joseph. The bond between sisters was tight, and particularly fond of Mary (who had married Lord Curzon), Daisy was close to her sister's middle child, Lady Cynthia, known as Cimmie. Daisy and her niece were faithful correspondents to one another, especially after Daisy had become a prolific letter-writer after her husband was killed in Mesopotamia during WWI.

Following the death of her mother, Mary, in 1906, Cimmie viewed her aunt as a confidant to whom she could go for advice. She sought no counsel from her domineering father and her self-centred, American stepmother, Grace. The relationship became especially poignant when she met and fell in love with Oswald Ernald Mosley (he would later be titled Sir after inheriting the baronetcy from his father in 1928), the dashing, youngest Conservative politician in the House.

On 11 May 1920, when Cimmie was 21, she married Mosley, her first and only lover. Their wedding took place in the Chapel Royal in St James's Palace in London. It was deemed the social event of the year with hundreds of guests attending, including King George V and Queen Mary, and various figure heads of European royalty.

Lord Curzon, her father, had taken some time to be persuaded that Mosley, later the founder of the British Union of Fascists, was a suitable husband for his free-spirited daughter who had Bolshevic tendencies. He suspected Mosley was largely motivated by social and political advancement, and, of course, Cimmie's inheritance from the Leiter trust-fund. He was right.

Mosley, known as Tom by his family and intimate friends, was the son of the reckless playboy and philanderer, Sir Oswald Mosley (the third cousin of the Earl of Strathmore, the father of Elizabeth Bowes-Lyon who served alongside King George VI as Consort of the United Kingdom), and the pious Maud, known as 'Ma'. Bolstering Mosley's ego, Maud thought her son was a God; her 'man-child', as she called him, which played a significant part in heightening Mosley's self-esteem. He failed to excel at school, though he did triumph in boxing, fencing and unsanctioned fistfights. His time at the Royal Military Academy Sandhurst was unremarkable, and he did not distinguish himself during the Great War, except to injure his leg while showing off to his mother and sister as he flew an aeroplane. His injury brought him a certain amount of credibility when he returned to the trenches before he was healed, inflicting on him a permanent limp. All his life he would suffer from phlebitis, a result of the wartime injury.

Mosley had fallen in love with Cimmie when they were both in Plymouth helping Nancy Astor in her campaign to become the first woman MP. Cimmie was attractive, approachable and, for a woman of that era, had an unusual interest in politics. Mosley, with his supreme self-confidence, was clearly the man Cimmie had been waiting for. Despite his appalling womanising, she remained submissively loyal to him. What she did say, or rather wailed, was *but they are all my best friends!*' when he admitted his dalliances with her female contemporaries. Though unknown to her, but common knowledge amongst his contemporaries, he had also slept with his sisters-in-law, Lady Irene Curzon (later Baroness Ravensdale) and Lady Alexandra 'Baba' Metcalfe, and his stepmother-in-law, Grace. Lord Curzon had quite rightly called his son-in-law a bounder, though he did not live long enough to see his prediction come to light.

As a young girl, Cimmie wrote in her diary that what she wanted above all else was 'a Big Solemn Comprehensive idea that holds you and me and all the world together in one great grand universal scheme'. When asking her father for permission to marry Mosley, she assured him, as Curzon wrote to Grace, that she and Mosley 'were going to have a great career together', and that 'he was destined to climb to the very top – with her aid'. Elinor Glyn, the famous society novelist and former mistress of Curzon, prophesied that having married Mosley, Cimmie would 'one day...rule England'. Cimmie's love-affair with the Labour Party at the time was little more than the fruit of her blind loyalty to Mosley. By 1932, she was just as enthusiastically extolling the merits of fascism.

In love, as in everything else, Mosley showed a marked preference for the swift attack. He proposed within a week of their meeting in Plymouth. Cimmie refused and went off on a skiing holiday, however, 3 months later, after going to bed with him, she accepted. In the first letter he ever wrote to her, Mosley said rather ominously: 'I would surrender the present with the ages to come and those past, just once to make you cry as I have made others cry; and then instead of leaving as I have always left tears, to kiss those tears away.' Their marriage, in which they had three children, lasted for 13 miserable years, blighted by not only his ongoing infidelity, but his passionate affair with Diana Mitford.

Succumbing to peritonitis in 1932, Cimmie died at the age of 34. The marriage to Mosley lasted until her death, though as her oldest child, Vivian, remarked: 'Peritonitis is what killed my mother, but with Diana there she didn't want to live.'

For information on Kerin Freeman's book *The Civilian Bomb Disposing Earl* visit www.pen-and-sword.co.uk. She can be contacted through her website www.kerinfreeman.webs.com

HOW I WAS INSPIRED TO WRITE THE LODGER

Words by Louisa Treger

Like many of the world's best discoveries, I stumbled on Dorothy Richardson by accident. I was researching Virginia Woolf for my PhD thesis in the London University library, when I found a review by Virginia about a writer whose name I did not recognise:

> Dorothy Richardson has invented ... a sentence which we might call the psychological sentence of the feminine gender. It is of a more elastic fibre than the old, capable of stretching to the extreme, of suspending the frailest particles, of enveloping the vaguest shapes ...

I was riveted. Who was Dorothy Richardson? How had she come to re-invent the English language, in order to record the experience of being a woman?

Further investigation led me to Dorothy's life work: the 12-volume autobiographical novel-sequence, *Pilgrimage*. I discovered that when the first volume came out in 1914, its innovative form sent shock-waves through the literary establishment. I began to read *Pilgrimage* with growing excitement, for here was someone of undoubted importance, now largely consigned to oblivion.

Dorothy's aim, in her own words, was to 'produce a feminine equivalent of the current masculine realism'. She felt that most novels were an expression of the vision, fantasies, and experiences of men, and that only rarely in the history of the novel could a genuine account of female experience be found. Her dissatisfaction led her to dispense with narrative conventions like plot, structure and narrator, and to seek a new, fluid way of writing that would render the texture of consciousness as it records life's impressions. The novelist May Sinclair coined the phrase 'stream of consciousness' to describe Dorothy's writing.

I became as captivated by Dorothy's life as I was by her books, for she was deeply unconventional in both. She was born in 1873, the third of four daughters. Her father came from a family who had made money through a grocery business, but he wanted to give up 'trade' and become a gentleman. He sold the family business and lived a cultivated and elegant life, until a series of unwise investments resulted in bankruptcy. In the wake of the disaster, Dorothy's mother became depressed. The family sent her on holiday with Dorothy to Hastings, but by this point, Mrs Richardson was beyond help. One day, while Dorothy was out for a walk, her mother committed suicide by cutting her throat with a kitchen knife. Dorothy was 22-years-old.

After the tragedy, Dorothy's family life broke up, and she moved to London, where she lived just above the poverty line in a Bloomsbury attic, and worked as a dentists' secretary for a salary of £1 per week. London at the beginning of the 20th century was a melting pot of societies and ideas, and Dorothy explored a wide variety of them, from the Conservative Primrose League to Russian anarchists, from Quakers to lectures on science and philosophy. It's during this period of her life that my novel is set. In the opening pages, Dorothy has just accepted an invitation to spend the weekend with an old school friend. Jane recently married a writer who is hovering on the brink of fame. His name is H.G. Wells, or Bertie, as he is known to friends.

Bertie Wells is short and unprepossessing, but Dorothy quickly notices his grey-blue eyes, looking at her with open approval. She notices his voice, which is high and husky, and the way his mind seethes with extraordinary ideas, like a volcano. He tells her that he and Jane have an agreement which allows them the freedom to take lovers, although Dorothy is sure her friend wouldn't be happy with this arrangement.

Tormented about betraying Jane, yet unable to draw back, Dorothy free-falls into an affair with Wells, and their relationship forms the heart of my novel. I don't want to go into detail about it, because I don't want to reveal too much about *The Lodger*, other than to say that Wells encouraged Dorothy to write, and her time with him shaped everything that happened afterwards.

Her career as an author began in the aftermath of the affair. The publication of the first volume of *Pilgrimage* was accompanied by a change in her personal life: she met her future husband, the artist Alan Odle. They rented rooms at the same boarding house in St John's Wood, and they fell into the habit of talking during breakfast.

Alan was extremely unusual. Picture a wraith-like figure, with long fair hair wound around his head, sharp ink-stained nails, and brown eyes that glowed with intelligence. Alan was tubercular; he was steadily drinking himself to death at the Café Royal in the company of artists like Aubrey Beardsley. Dorothy married him reluctantly, believing he had only 6 months to live.

Ironically, Alan survived for many years. Dorothy later made the wry comment: 'If I'd known we would both live to see our 25th wedding anniversary, I might have hesitated even more than I did...' Despite this, the marriage seems to have been a success.

Dorothy and Alan met and corresponded with some of the most interesting figures of their day. During a trip to Paris in the 1920s, for instance, they saw Ernest and Hadley Hemingway, Mary Butts and Cecil Maitland, Mina Loy, and others of the Montparnasse group. Hemingway begged Dorothy for a contribution to his new magazine *Transatlantic Review*, in which the opening of *Finnegan's Wake* had recently appeared. 'Please don't get English and say that you haven't anything that would be of use to us,' he implored, 'because I would be very happy to have any story of yours.' I think this little anecdote speaks volumes about how highly Dorothy was regarded.

However, the early recognition and interest in her writing gradually slid from her grasp. She blamed her 'failure' on the extra journalism she was forced to take on in order to earn a living, for neither her books nor Alan's drawings ever made money. For most of her adult life, she battled poverty in a series of shabby lodgings, her time eaten away by housework.

Dorothy died in poverty and obscurity. A visitor to the old age home where she spent her last years was told that Dorothy suffered from senile delusions: she thought she was a famous writer. To which her startled visitor replied, 'She *is* a famous writer!'

I found this anecdote unbearably poignant. It seemed tragic that this remarkable woman died unrecognised, and her work has been largely forgotten. I felt that people should know about her; that her story needed to be unearthed and retold. And this is how the idea for *The Lodger* was born.

🕊 Louisa Treger began her career as a classical violinist and worked as a freelance orchestral player and teacher. She subsequently turned to literature, gaining a PhD in English at University College London. Married with three children, she lives in London. *The Lodger* is her first novel.

Website: louisatreger.com
Twitter: @louisatreger
Facebook: https://www.facebook.com/louisatregerwriter

NANCY IN WARTIME

Words by Kim Place-Gateau

The beautiful, scandalous Mitford girls and their befuddled parents were political creatures to their cores. Volumes have been written about the often unsavoury, sometimes idealistic, occasionally noble, wildly divergent and always riveting ideologies possessed by this intelligent and determined family. It's entertaining to consider how emblematic their household dynamics and political disagreements were of the competing ideologies present in Britain in the 1930s and 1940s.

Let's start with an overview:

Unity's life was destroyed by Nazism and her devotion to Adolf Hitler.

Diana's reputation, family and health were all severely damaged by her allegiance to fascism. She rejected a life that was, by the standards of the day, perfect with enormous financial resources and a handsome, successful husband in order to dedicate herself to the British Union of Fascists and her beloved Sir Oswald Mosley.

Jessica ran away to America with her husband Esmond Romilly, who died fighting in the Royal Canadian Air Force in 1941. An enthusiastic communist since adolescence, she was one half of the polarising extremism that kept the Mitfords at odds for decades. By the end of World War II, Jessica had already become an American citizen.

Deborah was a traditionalist. An aristocrat to the core, she married the second son of the Duke of Devonshire. Eventually, and rather unexpectedly, she became one of the country's most popular duchesses, completely changing the way country houses are managed as she did so.

Tom was killed in the war in the Pacific, having refused to fight the Germans for political and personal reasons.

Pamela and her husband Derek Jackson were quiet supporters of Hitler for a time, but Jackson served bravely and with distinction during the war.

Lord and Lady Redesdale's marriage ended after the war. The loss of Tom and, after Unity's long and difficult convalescence, as well as Lady Redesdale's unrepentant Nazism, proved too much for Lord Redesdale to overcome.

And then there is Nancy. It is Nancy who most accurately represents the majority of the British public in this analogy. It is her perspective that won out, if you will, and was embraced by the majority of the country throughout the war. Like Britain itself, she managed to walk a fine line through the upheaval. She bent with the wind, overcame her weaknesses, and redefined who she was to become through her responses to the challenges of living in London during the war.

Her political perspective was shaped by her family, of course. How could anyone emerge from such a turmoil of arguments and competing loyalties without a firm grasp on how they see the world? But her political awakening came in France, as so many of her most significant experiences did for the rest of her life.

In 1939, Nancy joined her feckless husband Peter Rodd in Perpignan, where they both worked tirelessly to feed, clothe, shelter and eventually relocate thousands of Catalan refugees who had been displaced by the war in Spain. The scope of the indignities and misery Nancy saw while doing this difficult and emotionally draining work solidified her resolve against political extremism, and bolstered her socialist perspective. She wrote to her mother expressing just that: 'If you could have a look, as I have, at some of the less agreeable results of fascism in a country I think you would be less anxious for the swastika to become a flag on which the sun never sets.' To Mrs Hammersley, she was even more direct, taking a shot at communism as well: 'There isn't a pin to put between Nazis and Bloshies. If one is a Jew one prefers one & if an aristocrat the other, that's all as far as I can see. Fiends!' What Nancy lacked in nuance, she more than made up for in her determination thereafter to view the disastrous events of the day with common sense, and to maintain a vehement disdain for extreme political views.

Perpignan gave Nancy more than a political awakening, however. It gave her some moral high ground from which to judge her sisters (and plenty of material for Linda's adventures in her bestselling novel, *The Pursuit of Love*). Unlike Unity and Diana, she had taken tangible action. Though it could be argued that she was motivated to do this work by her desire to be near her wayward husband. From that point on she took action whenever she saw the need, independent of the men in her life. This, too, she saw as an important distinction between herself and her sisters.

She continued to take action. A summary of Nancy's work during WWII includes a brief stint as an air-raid protection driver. This wasn't her strong suit, and she was dismissed. Undaunted, she subsequently volunteered at a first aid station, performed admirably as a fire-watcher, and on three occasions in 1940, she protected and cared directly for people displaced by the war – a group of London evacuees who were sheltered at Peter's aunt's house in Hampshire, two children Peter brought home from a bombed-out house in Brixton, and, most extensively, at Rutland Gate, where Jewish families who had been evacuated from the industrial East End of London were billeted. These actions allowed Nancy to feel, with some justification, that rather than to simply make an unseemly fuss, and ally herself with horrifying men who had brought the situation they all faced into fruition, she had done her duty to attend to the results. She had done her part.

Nancy's role in Diana's incarceration is consistent with the world-view she had embraced. Unimaginable as this decision may seem, she simply did what she thought she must. 'Not very sisterly behaviour but in such times I think it one's duty?' she wrote to Mrs Hammersley, betraying a bit of inner conflict. Whatever doubts she may have had, she stayed true to her beliefs, and, duty attended to, carried on a merry correspondence with Diana throughout her incarceration at Holloway. All the while, she remained in London, despite the bombs, fires, chaos and danger.

Of course, Nancy wasn't without her flaws. Though her response to the war was, on the whole, admirable (her treachery regarding Diana being an exception) she continued to hold opinions that would not necessarily pass muster in contemporary Britain. But in contrast to her family, Nancy's pragmatism and moderate perspective represents a sort of essential Britishness that emerged and endured throughout the war. Regardless of this, she would leave England shortly after the war ended, never to live there again. She spent much of the remainder of her life in pursuit of an unattainable man, much as she had spent her youth.

None of this is to say that the other members of her family were not impacted by the horrors of the war; nothing could be further from the truth. But it was Nancy, the French Lady Writer, the Mitford who dedicated herself to France and the French, who was the most British of Mitfords when Britain was at war.

🖏 Kim Place-Gateau is a writer, entrepreneur and serial project starter who lives in Hawaii (but not for much longer) with her husband and many pets.

THE ADVENTURES OF ENID LINDEMAN

Words by Lyndsy Spence

Standing 6-feet-tall with handsome features and platinum hair, Enid Lindeman was never going to be a wallflower. As she gallivanted through life she accumulated four husbands, numerous lovers, and during the inter-war years her high-jinx dominated the gossip columns. Evelyn Waugh satirised her set in *Vile Bodies*, but the workings of his menacing imagination paled in comparison to the real thing.

Born in Australia in 1892, she was the great-granddaughter of Henry Lindeman, who founded Lindeman Wines in Hunter Valley, New South Wales. A privileged, if nondescript, childhood inspired Enid to look for a life of glamour and excitement. She achieved this at the age of 21 when she married Roderick Cameron, an American shipping magnate 24-years her senior. Establishing herself as a New York socialite, Enid would literally stop traffic ('the better to view this vision of perfection') when she emerged from the Cameron building in Manhattan. But the celebrated marriage was short-lived when, a year later, Cameron died from cancer, leaving his young wife a fortune of several million dollars.

The year was 1914 and the newly widowed Enid left New York with her 9-month-old son to move to Paris to drive an ambulance for the war effort. With her beauty, charm and charisma, she became popular with officers, and it was reported that five men, having found her so intoxicating, committed suicide. (One blew himself up; another threw himself under Le Train Bleu; another jumped overboard into shark infested waters). Or, as Enid put it, 'They were not able to take the strain.' An old boyfriend, Lord Derby, Britain's Minister for War, was concerned about the havoc she was causing amongst the officers and, hoping to tame her, he suggested she remarry. Although a millionairess in her own right, Enid was incapable of handling her finances and to ease this fiscal responsibility, she agreed. Derby produced her next husband, Brigadier General Frederick Cavendish, known as 'Caviar'.

After the war, Caviar was given command of the 9ᵗʰ Lancers in Egypt. As she had done in Paris, Enid caused a sensation amongst her husband's comrades in Cairo and, as a dare, she reportedly slept with his entire regiment. By day she schooled her husband's polo ponies and by night she dressed as a man to play with the band in the officers' mess hall. Cairo suited Enid's flamboyant tastes: there were picnics by the Nile, parties in sandstone mansions, and rides by moonlight in the Sahara. She met Lord Carnarvon (another of her lovers) on his famous dig of King Tutankhamen's tomb, and was one of the first to be taken down to the discovery.

In an attempt to distance Enid from hedonistic influences, Caviar took his wife, stepson and their two children to London, where the family moved into a townhouse in Mayfair. Domesticity never appealed to Enid, and she continued her pleasure-seeking ways in London's nightclubs. However, in 1931, she was once again a widow when Caviar died from a cerebral haemorrhage at their apartment in Paris.

In 1933, she met and married Marmaduke 'Duke' Furness, the 1st Viscount Furness, whose second wife, Thelma, was a lover of the Prince of Wales. (His first wife, Daisy, had died onboard his yacht and he buried her at sea). Although immensely rich with a private railroad car, two yachts and an aeroplane, Furness ordered Enid to sign over her personal fortune to him. Furness's London townhouse, Lees Place was not large enough 'to hide' Enid's three children from his sight, so she rented a flat on Curzon Street for the children and their staff. Suspicious that Enid was not being faithful, and intolerant to her platonic (a rarity) friendships with men, Furness hired detectives to watch her when he was at home and abroad. In spite of his jealousy, he showered her with expensive gifts and granted her every whim, one being exotic pets which included a tame cheetah, walked everyday by the children and their governess. She held court at Furness's villa, La Fiorentina, at Cap Ferrat in the south of France. A sensation wherever she went, it was said that people stood on chairs in the lobby of the Hotel de Paris in Monte Carlo just to catch sight of her as she passed through. Out of all her husbands, Enid claimed to love Furness the most: 'There was nothing in the world he was not prepared to give me. Of all the men who loved me, and some were as rich as Duke, he was the one who was prepared to lay the world at my feet.'

An enthusiastic gambler, Enid loved the races and casinos, and often carried a bag stuffed with £10 notes. Irresponsible with money, she squandered a fortune, and was as equally flippant with her jewels, keeping her pearls in Kleenex boxes because they were the closest thing to hand. She was also generous with money: if she saw ex-servicemen begging on the street or sitting on the pavement next to their watercolours for sale, she would order her chauffeur to stop the car, whereupon she would get out and offer them a job or find them a home. To the disapproval of Furness, she would take her children on jaunts to the suburbs to visit the ex-servicemen she had housed.

Furness died from cirrhosis of the liver in 1940. After his death, his former wife, Thelma, contested the will, claiming that their son should inherit his estate. After a long legal battle, Furness's eldest son (having been reported as missing in action) from his first wife was declared dead and the law sided with Thelma. Enid was not rewarded the money she had surrendered to Furness when they were married, but she was permitted to keep Lees Place in London. With the war raging around them, Enid and her daughter decamped to their villa in the south of France where they tended to prisoners from the detention camp near Eze. 2 years later, they escaped France and travelled to London by way of Portugal, where Enid used her influence to secure them passage on a flying boat.

In London, Enid was dubbed 'The Penniless Peeress' by the press. Down on her luck, she met Valentine Browne, the Earl of Kenmare, and famous gossip writer of the Londoner's Log (then known as Castlerosse because of his former title Viscount Castlerosse). The confidant and travelling companion of the press magnate Lord Beaverbrook, Valentine had lived an excessive life of debauchery, and had been a close friend and lover of Enid's when they both lived in Paris during WWI. Divorced from the scandalous courtesan Doris Delevingne, he was hoping for a more stable wife. They were married in 1943, and Enid became Lady Kenmare. An enormous gentleman who was reported to have sat on a dog and crushed it to death, Valentine's doctor warned Enid he had a weak heart and was to abstain from sex as it would surely kill him. She rejected the doctor's advice: 'It was one of the only pleasures left to him in life. How could I ration him?' He died of a heart attack less than a year after they were married. In her boldest move yet, Enid, at the age of 52, claimed she was pregnant and as such could hold onto the Kenmare estate until the potential heir was born. She kept up the charade for 13 months until the estate was eventually given to Valentine's nephew. Having buried four husbands, Somerset Maugham dubbed Enid, 'Lady Killmore'.

A chameleon to all men she fell in love with, Enid would become their ideal woman and his interests would become hers. As her wealth grew, through inheritance and marriages, her life became a grand production. All purchases centred around the bedchamber: there were silk sheets and embroidered silk and lace pillowslips (changed everyday), and nightgowns and negligees were bought in abundance. The bedroom, her natural habitat, was sprayed with liberal amounts of Patou's *Joy*, then costing three times more than any other scent, and her lady's maid was ordered to spray the nightgowns and negligees, as well as the bedclothes. Leaving the beside lamp on, the maid would then open the door to Enid's bathroom and fill the bath to a certain level with hot water and scent. Presumably Enid, whenever she returned, would add more hot water to it. However, Enid was never seen in bed with a man, not even her husband, for she considered that 'vastly improper'.

It was a role she knew well, and with copious amounts of money at her disposal, Enid played the part to perfection. Having outlived her lovers, in her later years she was revered as a society hostess amongst film stars, with her villa La Fiorentina becoming a hub for Hollywood royalty. She died in 1973 at the age of 81.

THE GIRL WHO BECAME MUV

Words by Lyndsy Spence

Born in 1880, Sydney's childhood was, as her daughters were apt to say, pathos personified. Her mother, Jessica, died after an ill-advised medical abortion, and at the age of 8, Sydney was left in the care of her eccentric father, Thomas Gibson Bowles, known as Tap. A keen sailor, Tap kept his two daughters with him whilst his two sons attended school. There was an 8-month voyage to the Middle East on his 150-tonne sailing schooner *Nereid*, where the motherless children weathered terrifying storms and were left to their own devices after their governess, Rita Shell, known as Tello, became incapacitated with seasickness. On their homeward journey, the schooner was almost wrecked in a hurricane off the coast of Syria when, against the advice of the port authorities in Alexandria, Tap set sail after he learned Tello was having an affair with a young naval officer. Returning to England in time for the election campaigns, Tap, a Conservative back-bench MP, bought a second yacht, the *Hoyden*, and made it his temporary home and campaign headquarters. During the parliamentary recess, the children joined their father for a sailing holiday to France. Aside from their sailing trips, Tap took his children on holidays to a rented house on Deeside, where he set up a Turkish bath in an empty dog kennel.

Tello did not accompany the children on their latter voyages, and for some years she disappeared from their lives. One day, Sydney spied Tello, accompanied by four young boys, walking down Sloane Street. It occurred to her that the eldest boy was the product of the affair in Alexandria, and she learned the other three were Tap's children. Tap had set her up in a house and made her editor of *The Lady*, the magazine he bought after the death of his wife. Sydney wondered why Tap never married Tello, and concluded it must have been because the eldest boy was not his.

Tap's unique ideas on parenting were the norm for Sydney and her siblings. The nursery rules would influence the way she raised her own seven children; they were to adhere to a strict mosaic diet, they were not to be forced to eat anything they disliked, windows were to be left open 6-inches all year round, and after their bath they were to be rinsed with clean water. He did not believe in spoiling the children and they were not given Christmas or birthday presents; he reminded them that he 'housed, fed, watered, clothed and educated them and that was enough'. Unlike men of his generation, he was an attentive father, and when in London, he and Sydney rode everyday in Rotten Row. He sent the girls to skating lessons at the Prince's Club, the ice-rink at Montpelier Square, where Sydney fell in love with her instructor, Henning Grenander, a Swedish champion figure-skater. 'I would do almost anything he asked me,' she wrote in her diary. 'I would let him call me Sydney, I would even let him kiss me…'

At the age of 14, Tap had appointed Sydney as housekeeper of his London townhouse at 25 Lowndes Square, whereupon she developed a lifelong mistrust of male servants; she found them drunken and unreliable. The butlers and footmen were amused by this tall, angular young girl dressed in a thick serge sailor suit. The sailor suit was worn everyday, and for years Tap thought it appropriate for all occasions, until a lady friend suggested he should buy his 18-year-old daughter some decent clothes befitting her age and her social standing.

In 1894, still aged 14, Sydney accompanied her father to visit his good friend, Lord Redesdale, at his country house, Batsford. It was at Batsford that she first met Lord Redesdale's son, David Freeman-Mitford, who, at the age of 17, was classically handsome with bright blue eyes, blonde hair and a tanned complexion. Dressed smartly in an old brown velveteen keeper's jacket, he stood in the vast library with his back to the fire, and one foot casually resting on the fender. At that moment, Sydney wrote in an unpublished memoir, she lost her heart.

The infatuation with David was short-lived, for he went off to Ceylon hoping to earn a fortune as a tea-planter. Sydney herself was busy growing up, and 4 years later she came out as a debutante. Highly intelligent and possessing domestic capabilities, rare for a woman of her standing, there was talk of sending her to Girton, the women's college at Cambridge. However, for an unknown reason, the idea was not pursued. There were romantic relationships too, the first ending in tragedy when the young man was killed in the Boer War.

David's tea-planting venture was unsuccessful, and having spent less than 4 years in India, he returned home and enlisted in the Royal Northumberland Fusiliers to fight in the Boer War. In 1902, he was badly injured in his chest and lost a lung. Nursed for 4 days in a field hospital, he dictated a love letter, to be given to Sydney in the event of his death. When it was evident he would live, he was carried back to camp in a bullock cart, his wound swarming with maggots.

Having lost a boyfriend in the war, Sydney was sympathetic to David, whom she had sporadic contact with throughout the years. After he was invalided home, their meetings became more frequent, and David fell in love with her. However, Sydney was involved with another young man, Edward 'Jimmy' Meade, whose proposal she almost accepted, but the relationship ended in 1903 when she discovered he was a womaniser.

There were whispers in society that Sydney accepted David's proposal on the rebound from Jimmy Meade. They were married in 1904, 10 years after Sydney first saw him at Batsford. And, as they say, the rest is history…

THAT MITFORD THING IN US

Words by Virginie Pronovost

Six girls, six sisters, six mythic women: Nancy, Pamela, Diana, Unity, Jessica and Deborah. The Mitford sisters. They were all famous for different reasons, some being better known than the other, depending on their lifestyle. They certainly became one of the most popular group of sisters.

However, it's unfortunate that not everybody has the privilege of knowing of them. I, for instance, used to know nothing about them, until I read *The Mitford Girls' Guide to Life*. I have always been interested in British culture (cinema, music, literature), so to read a book about the six Mitford girls was certainly a must.

I have no doubt that most people living in the UK will know of the Mitford Girls, or have heard about them. They are, for better or worse, part of British culture. But for someone, who, like me, lives in Quebec, they might not necessarily be interested by the British culture. As a result, he or she has probably never heard of the Mitfords, even less if they are young. Well, I'll give you an idea of whom I'm talking about: my young, 20-something French-Canadian friends. Of course, when I told my friends that I was reading a book about the Mitford girls, their first question was to ask: 'Oh, who are they?' After my quick explanation, I feel they now know a little more about them, but are they really interested and curious about the girls?

Let's make them forget the various celebrity sister acts. We need to bring today's young people on a time travel and make them realise how they could identify themselves with the Mitford girls. Actually, I think each person, from any generation, can identify with one, two or three of the Mitfords.

Before I explore this subject more deeply, let's understand where my knowledge for those historical women springs from. However, I'm not a Mitford specialist, as they are just a new discovery to me. When I read about the girls, I was amazed by them. I must say, I'm not a fan of Diana and Unity's politics (they were both Nazi/Fascist sympathisers), but I think that each girl has something interesting and, as a group, they compliment one other very well. It's also hard for me to say who is my favourite Mitford girl. Maybe Pamela. She would be a favourite for many people. She was so lovable. Impossible not to like her. Unfortunately, unlike her other sisters, she had a much more quiet life, so there isn't so much to tell about her.

The Mitford girls had qualities and faults, like everybody else. Then, what would be the perfect Mitford girl? She would have Diana's beauty, Pamela's wisdom, Unity's passion (not necessarily for Hitler), Nancy's good tastes for fashion and cleverness, Jessica's devotion and open-mindedness, and Deborah's goodwill. But, only one Mitford girl is not nearly as thrilling as six of them!

The Mitford girls were not common individuals. They were not like every British citizen of the twentieth century. They were 'modern'. That is why we can easily identify ourselves to them. As I was reading about them, I realised that, in a group of friends, each person could be represented by one of the Mitford girls. Or, in a more general way, each sister could represent a certain group of persons, depending on their characteristics. That's why I decided to concentrate myself, not on what they did to influence the course of history, but on how they were as individuals. What makes Jessica Mitford so different from Unity Mitford? Why is Pamela the most loved Mitford girl? Why are Diana and Unity are so misunderstood? All these questions can help us to place the Mitford girls in our modern society and include them amongst the public personalities of my generation.

We can now ask ourselves how the Mitford girls would be represented in a group.

Every group needs a leader, and Nancy Mitford would be the perfect girl for this role. Nancy is the kind of person we admire because she has success and good tastes. To me, Nancy seemed to be the most self-confident of the six Mitford girls, and that is a perfect quality for a chief. Born in 1904, she became a famous novelist, particularly known for *The Pursuit of Love* and *Love in a Cold Climate*. Nancy would represent the group leader also because of her strong personality.

Pamela, known as 'the quiet Mitford', is the one in the group who rarely had problems with the others as she doesn't get angry easily. Even her looks, blonde with blue eyes, seemed to inspire peace. Wise, smiling and calm, she remains discreet, but her presence is always appreciated. As a person, Pamela might be a little vulnerable. We can think of Pamela's purposely induced miscarriage at the hands of her husband, Derek Jackson, because he didn't like children. Finally, as Pamela loved animals, she could represent the healthy-living person of the group. There is always one.

Diana Mitford, the prettiest Mitford girl, and Unity Mitford could be grouped together. In a group, those two would represent the ones who made bad choices or who act too fast. They are the most misunderstood persons because of their tastes and ideologies. Unfortunately for them, the result is not always the one they had hoped for. Diana and her husband, Sir Oswald Mosley, were both imprisoned because of their affiliation with Hitler and participation in the

British Union of Fascists. Unity, a great admirer of Hitler, couldn't stand the fact that Germany and England were at war against one other and she tried to commit suicide. It failed and she never was the same after. The Unity Mitford person is not necessarily a Nazi sympathizer, but her ideas make her maybe less appreciated and more vulnerable. However, people will always try to understand her the best they can. The Diana and Unity persons are those who live as they please. They think they need nobody to guide their life, but they could be wrong.

Of course, each group of friends needs a rebellious person. Jessica Mitford would, without a doubt, represent this one. This communist writer and journalist was the sister who wanted to change the world and make it a better place. She first ran away from home to help in the Spanish Civil War, and then lived in America where she fought for Civil Rights. The Jessica person always participates in good causes; she fights for her convictions, she might write about it for a publication, or several. For that, she might be greatly admired, but has to face her rivals: the Unity and Diana persons.

Finally, Deborah Mitford, or the Duchess of Devonshire, would represent the most helpful person of the group. She knows how to listen to other people's problems and give them wise advice without judging. I felt like Deborah was perhaps the most understanding of the six girls. Deborah was also a huge fan of Elvis Presley. We all know someone around who idolises some singer or celebrity. That would be the Deborah person of the group.

A group represented by the six Mitford girls can't be anything but fascinating, especially because of their differences. Can you identify yourself with one of the Mitfords? Can you think of someone who is just like Jessica Mitford or like Nancy Mitford? Many persons could have Pamela's behavior, but the Mitford girls were notorious for their achievements. It's not really how they were that made them famous, or infamous, but how they decided to use their personalities. However, that is something we can't steal from them, and that is why they are so unique.

🏛 Virginie Pronovost was born in Montreal, Canada on 3 April 1995. She is passionate about cinema and studied it at the college André-Grasset, and did a screen writing certificate at the University of Quebec in Montreal. She is now doing a major in Film Studies at Concordia University in Montreal. She expresses her love of classic cinema on her blog The Wonderful World of Cinema, and writes movie reviews for the website ClassicFlix. Virginie also loves literature and is fascinated by British culture, which explains her interest in the Mitford Girls.

SOCIETY STAR:

THE LIFE AND TIMES OF VISCOUNTESS MASSEREENE

Words by Lyndsy Spence

Before she became chatelaine of Antrim Castle at the age of 21, having married the 12th Viscount Massereene, Jean Barbara Ainsworth was a society star. Standing 6-feet-tall with black hair and dark eyes, her exotic looks attracted attention from both sexes. Women admired her avant garde fashion sense – she was always something of a style icon – and her penchant for flamboyant clothes, during the Edwardian era, was displayed through backless dresses, bejewelled head-wear and a long string of pearls tied in a knot. Her clothing was daring, as was her behaviour, and men admired her willingness to speak her mind. After a summer of parties in the salons of Mayfair and hunt balls in stately homes, she met her future husband, Algernon William John Clotworthy Skeffington. They married in February 1905, and 3 months later Algernon succeeded his father as the 12th Viscount Massereene and 5th Viscount Ferrard.

It was a glamourous marriage, reported in the stylish magazines of the day: *Tatler*, *The Bystander* and *The Sketch*. With her new husband, 12-years her senior and a war hero (Lord Massereene served with the 17th Lancers in the Boer War and was mentioned in Dispatches twice), Lady Massereene had become a celebrity. It was an age when the merits of stardom were weighed against one's background and breeding, and regardless of her title, she was a prime candidate during this new wave of modern media, much like today. She was born in Scotland in 1884, the eldest daughter of Sir John Stirling Ainsworth (he was given a peerage in 1917), a wealthy industrialist, banker and Liberal politician. She had grown up accustomed to large houses with staff, fascinating house-guests from the political and industrial worlds, and the privileges her father's money could afford her.

The political element would conjure up discord between father and daughter, for, in 1910, Lord and Lady Massereene allayed themselves with Edward Carson to resist Home Rule. John Ainsworth was a Home Ruler, and he accused Lord Massereene of influencing his daughter. But nobody could tell her what to do, and she threw herself into the Unionist cause. The Massereene seat, Antrim Castle, a 17th century dwelling overlooking the parish of Antrim, became a refuge for Carson and his Antrim branch of the Ulster Volunteer Force (UVF). The Massereenes land became a parade ground for the UVF, where, after militant marches and various displays of pageantry, Lady Massereene inspected the men. Afterwards she passed out cigarettes, known as 'smokes', and gave rousing speeches to the local supporters. The UVF was breaking the law by holding armed events, and Lady Massereene, a participant in their illegal activity, would soon suffer the consequences. A rumour spread through Antrim that Lord Massereene had been arrested and that Carson was at the castle. In a letter to her friend Edith, Lady Londonderry, she described how the rumour had provoked an 'angry' and 'over-zealous' crowd to follow the housekeeper who was manhandled in an attempt to retrieve information.

Far from defeated by the heightened tensions in the town, Lady Massereene founded a corps of nurses, named the Volunteer Aid Attachment Corps. The training consisted of 5 weeks with the Red Cross or St John Ambulance to ensure the women were equipped to care for volunteers if they went into battle. A dressing station was established in Randalstown, while Antrim Castle and the O'Neill seat, Shane's Castle, were on standby to be transformed into clearing hospitals.

On Easter Monday of 1914, Carson returned to Antrim Castle during his task to review 2,800 volunteers from the three south Antrim battalions. A luncheon was given in his honour, and amongst the UVF hierarchy were a countess, a marquis, a duchess and various lords and ladies. A photograph exists of Lord and Lady Massereene standing on the steps of Antrim Castle with Carson and his cronies. Afterwards, Carson inspected the nursing corps, led by Lady Massereene on a swarm facing the castle and comprised of 80 members from Antrim, Randalstown, Lisburn, Glenavy and Crumlin. Prayers were followed by the formal dedication of the UVF's colours, made by the Lord Bishop. Lady Massereene presented Carson with the King's colour and the regimental colour of the battalion, a personal gift from her.

There were no women in local government and Lady Massereene was a rare female voice in public life. Her views on women's role in society were made clear when, opening a Bazaar in Dunadry in aid of Muckamore New Schools, she referred to the topical Suffragette movement. The school's colours of green, blue and orange, were Suffragette colours, and she joked that if any such ladies were presented they should not begin 'operations by destroying the new schools', before adding: 'I believe in the higher education of women – the reason was that education makes them much better wives and mothers. The future of the empire depended to a very large extent, if not altogether, upon the mental training of mothers, and the way in which they brought up their children.' The speech was an example of her chameleon-like tendencies to appeal to whichever crowd she was addressing.

The arrival of WWI in 1914 saw Lady Massereene move out of her husband's shadow and into a role that was entirely her own. Lord Massereene went to the front with the North Irish Horse, and there had been scenes of enthusiasm from the locals as he went to Antrim railway station on 8 August for France. Accompanied by Lady Massereene and their daughter, Diana, born in 1909, the Massereene Brass and Reed Band played a number of patriotic tunes on the platform as the train departed.

This was the era in which Lady Massereene's charity work came to the forefront, and divided locals seemed to forget about her allegiance with Carson. At home, she joined a distress committee aimed at helping dependents of soldiers and sailors who had gone to war. In October 1914, Lady Massereene's second child, a son and heir, was born while Lord Massereene was in France. A month after the birth of her son, Lady Massereene hosted a successful fancy dress ball at the Protestant Hall. The fundraiser was for an ambulance, which she planned to send out to the front. Her war work continued in London, where she had been made Commandant of Women's League's Canteens, and dressed in her usual flamboyant style, a group of soldiers mistook her for a streetwalker and asked if she had had much luck at Piccadilly the night before. With her usual good humour, she laughed it off and relayed the anecdote for years to come. She trained as a nurse and volunteered at London hospitals, tending to the wounded. By chance, Lady Massereene along with other aristocratic nurses appeared as themselves, albeit in uniform, in the 1918 Hollywood silent film, *The Great Love*, starring Lilian Gish.

Lady Massereene's postwar life saw her re-emerge on the social scene, and Sir John Lavery painted her portrait, a macabre study in black that, in hindsight, foretold the tragedies that were to come. On 28 October 1922, Antrim castle held a grand ball, after which a fire broke out. Guests tried to extinguish the fire, to no avail, and locals rallied to the castle, concentrating their efforts on rescuing the servants whose quarters were 50-feet above the ground. Lady Massereene fled to the nursery to rescue her children, and trapped on a stairwell engulfed by smoke, she warned them they might not live. They watched as their cat caught on fire and perished before their eyes. Eventually, Lt Col Stewart Richardson, a war veteran who was staying at the castle, saved the lives of Lady Massereene and her children by tying sheets together and lowering them down from the roof of the chapel.

In 1923, a claim was made, and eventually rejected, for £90,000 worth of malicious damage. Damning evidence was presented before the court in Belfast, including a paraffin barrel that was full before the fire and now found to be empty. The windows of the basement were also discovered to be forced open, thus allowing the flames to spread more quickly. Anonymous letters, too, were touched upon (she showed her husband but not the police) in which Lady Massereene was warned she would soon 'meet her maker'. Such letters were sent in retaliation to Lady Massereene's pro-Unionist speeches in which she said: 'Let's arm ourselves that Ulster will never surrender an inch of her soil or title of right to the insidious bloody foe.' The Massereenes believed the fire was started intentionally as the castle did not burn down as a result of a single fire. The water supply in the cisterns had been tampered with and several items that had been saved from the fire were found to be covered in mineral oil. During the investigation, Lady Massereene was questioned about the repairs that had been carried out on the fireplaces. She replied that, owing to a dream she had had 10 years previously that a fire had broken out in her boudoir, she made a conscious effort to have the grate in her bedroom replaced.

This was not the first time Lady Massereene relied on or spoke openly about her dreams. A decade before, her tiara was stolen from the castle and she ordered the police to comb the banks of the Six Mile River, having dreamt it was discarded there. She was, in fact, the victim of a network of jewel thieves who were eventually caught in London and arrested. She harboured a deep interest in the paranormal and was renowned in London as a ghost expert. A close friend of the society spiritualist Violet Tweedale, Lady Massereene related her paranormal experiences in Tweedale's book *Ghosts I Have Seen*. She also spoke openly to various London newspapers about her psychic abilities and affiliation with the spirit world.

In 1930, Lady Massereene suffered a bitter blow when her eldest child and only daughter Diana Skeffington died suddenly at the age of 21 after contracting typhoid at a wedding in Scotland. Lord and Lady Massereene never recovered from their daughter's death, and having once spoke enthusiastically about rebuilding a country house on the site of the castle, Lord Massereene lost interest. They went their separate ways though never divorced, with Lord Massereene residing in apartments at Clotworthy House and Lady Massereene living in London, where in place of her once grand house parties she hosted seances. Many believed her obsession with the supernatural was a source of comfort to her after Diana's death.

Lady Massereene's final years were plagued by illness, although she never believed she was seriously ill. After collapsing in Hyde Park, she went up to Knock House, her Scottish residence in Mull, where her condition deteriorated. 5 week later, in the winter of 1937, she died at the age of 54. Having championed the existence of ghosts, many of whom she called friends, one assumes, and hopes, Lady Massereene languishes in that spiritual realm.

VIRGINIA DURR AND THE ROMILLYS

Words by Leia Clancy

'Old Virginny, don't you think you could keep dear Decca while I'm gone? If you will just keep her for the weekend, I can't tell you how I would appreciate it.'

Virginia Durr had no intention of agreeing to Esmond Romilly's request. She was about to leave for the Democratic Convention in Chicago where she would need to 'politick' and present on the anti-poll tax bill. She did not want Decca to go with her. Of course Esmond, as always, won Virginia over and Decca joined her on the long drive from Washington DC to Illinois. Almost immediately after setting out on the journey, Decca stopped the car so she could go to the lavatory. This happened every 15 minutes; she simply *had* to use the lavatory. The driver was furious: 'That girl has a weak bladder; we'll never get to Chicago.' The next time Decca stopped the car, a suspicious Virginia followed her and discovered Decca did not have a weak bladder at all; she simply had morning sickness.

Decca planned to go back to New York after the convention and get another job in a dress shop, but Virginia insisted: 'You can't go if you're still throwing up so much. You stay here until you get over being sick.'

Decca lived in the Durr household for nearly 3 years.

Against all odds, Virginia Durr was at the heart of the American civil rights movement. Born in Birmingham, Alabama in 1903, she grew up in a traditional Southern family who firmly believed in the value of slavery and segregation. Her education at Wellesley College awoke her; she was outraged by their rotating table rules. Why should she have to eat at the same table as a black student? Virginia realised soon enough that her outrage was foul and entirely baseless. She had loved her childhood nurse, a black woman, so much, and had often hugged and kissed her, so why was she so upset at the thought of eating with a black student? From then on, Virginia questioned the values she had been raised with.

A few years after leaving Wellesley, Virginia met and married Clifford Durr, a prominent lawyer. Their move to Washington DC led them both to become actively involved in civil rights. Clifford joined the Reconstruction Finance Corporation, a government organisation set up to help banks and businesses after the Great Depression. After meeting Eleanor Roosevelt in Washington, Virginia decided to volunteer for the Women's Division of the National Democratic Committee and distinguished herself from other southern belles by delving headfirst into Democratic politics. She dedicated herself to abolishing the poll-tax, a tax designed to prevent southern African Americans from voting. She continued tirelessly with this work for more than 20 years.

Virginia and Clifford Durr met Esmond and Decca Romilly at a cocktail party in 1940. Decca's first impression of Virginia was her 'soft scream' of a voice and inclination to fire question after question at her guests; Decca was overwhelmed by her directness. Esmond's stories of the Spanish Civil War had a profound effect on Virginia as she shared their disappointment that the US had not intervened. Decca attributed their quick intimacy with each other to American openness, but the truth was that they had plenty in common. They were fiercely opinionated, impassioned by social justice, and unafraid of going against the grain. It was their affection for each other that Esmond depended on when he asked Virginia to take care of Decca.

Shortly after the eventful visit to the Democratic Convention, they received a letter from Oxford University where Clifford Durr had been a Rhodes Scholar. Oxford professors and their wives were being sent over to America and the University asked if the Durrs could take care of a Mrs Woozley and her baby. Despite already filling their home with their own three children, a pregnant Decca and occasional visiting parents, the Durrs agreed. Mrs Woozley assured them that she would be no trouble at all, but she would need a private room and bath, and they would need to find her a nanny. Virginia could see that Mrs Woozley might actually be quite a lot of trouble and advised Decca that she would have to leave once Mrs Woozley arrived. But as fate would have it, Mrs Woozley followed her demands with another letter, informing them that due to torpedoing in the Atlantic, she would try her luck in Oxford. Decca volunteered to be their 'refugee' instead.

Decca's time with the Durrs was defined by the death of Esmond in 1941. This devastating event is marked with a footnote in *Hons and Rebels*. In her memoirs, Virginia recounted the profoundly shattering effect this loss had on Decca, remembering her overwhelmed by grief and suffering from nightmares about Esmond's drowning. Decca was never known for displaying emotion and even Virginia wrote about her ability to 'freeze the marrow of people's bones'. With this in mind, she acknowledged that she was one of the very few to have seen the real, vulnerable Decca.

After Esmond's death, Decca had to begin her life again and was able to do so because of the Durrs deep affection and support. It was through Virginia and Clifford that Decca met so many New Dealers and was able to build a happy and fulfilling social life amongst them. Through them, Decca had a front row seat to the civil rights work taking place in Washington DC and though she eventually left the city, she never lost touch with the Durrs.

Likewise, Virginia and Clifford left Washington to return to Montgomery, where the civil rights movement was just beginning to take shape. The Durrs continued their work against desegregation, becoming well acquainted with key civil rights figures like Martin Luther King, E D Nixon and Rosa Parks. The Durrs and Nixon were the ones to pay Parks's bail when she was arrested for failing to give up her bus seat. They became intimately involved in fighting for civil rights in the south, and Virginia's persistent work to abolish the poll tax succeeded in 1965 with the passing of the Voting Rights Act.

The Durrs may appear to be relatively minor characters in the fantastically sprawling Mitford story, but the reality is far from it. Their support and guidance to Decca was significant and being enveloped by Virginia's confident, politicised presence arguably steered her towards a more active, political future. Had Virginia been less kind, less southern, or less hospitable, Decca may have ended up back in New York, working in a dress shop.

✄ Leia Clancy lives in London. Decca is her favourite Mitford sister.

THE MAVERICK MOUNTAINEER

Words by Robert Wainwright

When a 13-year-old boy chased a mob of wallaby up Mt Canobolas on the outskirts of the inland New South Wales town of Orange one spring morning in 1901 he could not have imagined that his climb would be the precursor to one of the great pioneering adventures of modern times – and lead him to the roof of the world.

That day, George Finch, a rangy and steely-eyed Australian youth, stood in wonderment at the land stretched before him and decided then and there that he wanted to see the world from atop its highest vantage point. Along the way he would challenge the hostile demands of the British establishment which would not take kindly to a vocal and maverick colonial youth who wore his hair long, spoke German and climbed alpine peaks with modern equipment and without the traditional professional guides.

But this intriguing polymath and anti-hero was inspired by more than just the physical world. Intrigued by the wooden 18th century instrument designed to demonstrate Newton's law of motion in his father's library, George would also become a scientist of pioneering the use of bottled oxygen at altitude, and designing a jacket made of balloon fabric and eiderdown stuffing that would be the forerunner of today's ubiquitous puffer jacket.

He would twice be decorated a war hero, once as a soldier in the Great War and then as a civilian helping London resist the Blitz of 1941, he helped unravel the mysteries of metals that would improve the efficacy of the combustion engine, build a camera to inspect microscopic electrons and be involved in the synthesis of ammonia from air that would allow manufacture of fertilizer in commercial quantities.

So who was this man, and why has his extraordinary life gone largely unrecognised?

George Ingle Finch was born in 1888, in a stone homestead on the sheep and cattle station established by his grandfather 170 miles inland from Sydney. A self-made man from an English village near Cambridge, Charles Wray, George sailed to the colonies as a soldier but quickly worked hard to become a prominent landowner, farmer and politician. However it was George's father Charles Edward, who deeply inspired his young son, encouraging early independence and freedom to explore the untamed wilds of his inland home while stirring the young man's interest in the mysteries of science.

The combination was irresistible when the family sailed to Europe in 1902 for what was supposed to be a yearlong tour but instead became their new home, led by George's bohemian mother Laura. As much as Charles Finch was a straight-laced man of 60, his much younger wife longed to shed the boredom of an Australian bush life and insisted on settling in Paris. Even when Charles returned home to New South Wales, Laura stayed with her three children – George the eldest, brother Max, and sister Dorothy. The boys would never see their father again.

From their first climbing adventure – scaling Notre Dame Cathedral by moonlight – George and Max would challenge authority and convention, their enthusiasm for alpine peaks slowed only by their mother who insisted on height limits and teachers who instilled the need for honing skills with icepick and rope, patience and careful planning on the pair. It suited George's logical brain and would be one of the few times in his life that he accepted the advice of others over his own intuition.

Having struggled through his early school years and rejected medical studies at the Sorbonne, he found an academic home at the Zurich Institute of Technology where, after managing to become fluent in Swiss-German within 6 months, he studied physical sciences, not only passing but winning the university's gold medal. Albert Einstein was among his tutors.

Weekends and summer holidays were largely spent with younger brother, Max, exploring the Alps, travelling by train to villages in Switzerland, Italy and France and then hiking to ramshackle mountain huts from where they would launch audacious assaults on peaks such as the Eiger, Matterhorn, Monte Rosa, and dozens of others, often leaving in the early hours of the morning to avoid the inevitable avalanches cause by the morning sun. Their great joy was sitting atop a peak, boiling a brew of tea by melting snow on a small stove and sharing tins of peaches drenched in condensed milk.

The Finch boys however were different as climbers, passionate and at home with nature and uninterested in the established practice of paying local guides to lead them up the mountain's easiest lines of ascent. Instead, they chose the tougher routes, challenging themselves often on the steeper north faces of the giants that had rarely – or in some cases – never been conquered.

Their exuberant exploits brought them head to head with the tweed-jacketed, pipe-smoking gentlemen of London's stitched up Alpine Club of Savile Row. These aging, often arrogant men were founding members of the 'golden age' of mountaineering when Europe's Alpine peaks were climbed one after another, usually led by paid local guides.

George Finch's audacious climbs, leading strong if inexperienced climbers up dangerous ascents using new technology including silk ropes, pitons and better designed ice axes, incurred the wrath of the Alpine Club, often in print back in London. George, already recognised as the leading climber of his generation, would fire back with gusto, equally publicly. In one particularly barbed salvo published in 1913 in the English sports magazine, *The Field,* George didn't hold back:

> A man who climbs consistently with guides may be a great mountaineer but he need be nothing more than a good walker to 'climb' any peak in the Alps. The man who has to depend on his own skill, strength and nerve must have the craft at his finger-ends. The guided mountaineer need only follow patiently in the footsteps of a guide. He may and often does climb for years without the power to lead up easy rocks, to cut steps in ice, or find a route up an easy snow route. In the early days mountaineering, because of its expense, was almost exclusively the luxury of men who had made a position in life. It was controlled by men to whom years had brought prudence, men who looked with suspicion on enterprise beyond traditional limits.

> It is no longer the monopoly of rich Englishmen. The younger men are taking up the sport and gradually coming to the front. The development of guideless climbing has brought the Alps within reach of young men with limited means. For good or evil, guideless parties composed of young Englishmen are becoming more and more common. The attitude of the older climbers is changing. The spirit that saw the Alps a preserve for moneyed and middle-aged Englishmen is dead.

That article would come to define a large part of his life battling both mountains and men.

London certainly beckoned in 1913, not least because George could sense that war with Germany was now not just a possibility but a likelihood. He had witnessed the growing instability inside the country where he had been working as a research assistant and then factory foreman, helping to turn the theory of producing ammonia from oxygen into the reality of the commercial production of fertilizer. The project he worked on would earn two men, Fritz Haber and Carl Bosch, Nobel Prizes, and come to be regarded as one of the most important industrial breakthroughs of the 20th century.

George was nearing his 25th birthday when he arrived in the British capital, a young man already known for his mountaineering exploits but perfectly happy to enter the anonymous world of teaching at London's Imperial College. His fears came to fruition a year later when the Great War erupted. George volunteered soon after but he would not see action until 1916 when he was sent not to France, as expected, but the Balkans front at Salonika.

Here, amid the heat and disease of the eastern stalemate, he would make a name for himself, firstly for coordinating the repair of thousands of missiles that had been made useless by the heat melting the seals. George and a small team were forced to take apart and then reseal the arsenal, piece-by-piece, using a temporary wax seal devised by a young Australian scientist.

But it was an ingenious device to thwart an ace German pilot that brought George fame. In September 1917, 21-year-old Rudolf Von Eschwegge, the Red Baron of the Balkans, as he was known, was creating havoc on the frontline. He was more skillful and better equipped than the British pilots he faced, and even shot down observation balloons. George rigged the basket of one balloon with 500lb of booby-trapped explosives, triggering it from the ground with a hand held detonator as 'The Eagle' attacked the balloon. George was awarded a military MBE, presented by King George V, after the war had ended.

But as he reveled in the limelight, George Finch's personal life was unraveling. A few months after signing up he had met and swiftly married Betty Fisher, an attractive, vampish young woman from London. But within weeks of leaving for the front, Betty embarked on an adulterous affair with a Poona Horse officer named Wentworth 'Jock' Campbell.

When George was called back to London in early 1917 he found Betty nursing a baby boy. Peter Finch would grow up to be a famous Hollywood actor but died in 1977 still unsure of which man was his father, a frustration echoed in final role as Howard Beal in the movie *Network*, in which he played the angry newsroom executive who was 'as mad as hell and I'm not going to take it anymore'. The performance would earn him the first posthumous Academy Award for best actor.

In his fury at his wife's infidelity, George found and thrashed Campbell, and made Betty promise to cease the affair. She agreed but then renewed the relationship. In the resulting divorce, George took Peter, then 2-years-old, and sent him to his own mother, Laura, to be raised. Betty, pregnant again, would marry Jock although it was not to last. She would deliver another son, named Michael, who would spend his life also wondering about his father.

In the meantime George had met and fallen in love with a nurse who had helped him back to health following a bout of wartime malaria. But the infatuation with Gladys May would fade after the war ended and mountaineering resumed. He returned from a climbing trip in 1919 to end the relationship only to find that Gladys was pregnant. In a naive effort to save her from the shame of a child out of wedlock, he went ahead with the marriage, only to leave her a few weeks later. This time he would not take the baby – another son named Bryan – but promised financial support.

Perhaps it was the war that shook his usual emotional sure-footedness but George then reached the darkest time of his life. Two failed marriages and two sons – he was unlikely to have even known about Michael – were taking their toll on his spirit until he met a vivacious and intelligent young Scotswoman named Agnes Johnston. George would fall in love with the woman he called Bubbles and this time the marriage would last, eventually producing three daughters, two of whom are still alive.

There would be another huge event that would change his life: the chance to climb Mount Everest. In 1919, the Tibetan Government decided to lift the longtime ban on foreigners entering the only known route to the highest point on earth, Chomolungma, Mother Goddess of the World.

No European had been within 100 kilometres of the mountain, let alone attempted to climb it. Conquering Everest wasn't just about the adventurous spirit of man, but saving the face of the British Empire which had been beaten to both poles: to the south by Norwegian Roald Amunsden and the north by American Robert Edwin Peary. The Alpine Club and the Royal Geographical Society joined forces to create the Everest Committee and jointly chose a team, first to make a reconnaissance expedition in 1921 and the following year to attempt an ascent.

The two most obvious candidates as lead climbers were George Mallory and George Finch, two very different men in thought and behavior but the perfect foil for one another – one a rock climber of balletic poise and the other a methodical man of ice and snow who scaled the Alps like a spider. But while Mallory was a Cambridge man and a darling of the British establishment, George Finch was the opposite; an antipodean upstart, educated on the Continent and who loved nothing more than challenging convention.

The man who most hated George Finch was a Cambridge mathematician named Arthur Hinks, a brilliant but bitter man who served as secretary to the RGS and the Everest Committee. Hinks hated anything modern including the telephone, and George, to him, embodied modernity.

It was only because of the support of Percy Farrar, the charismatic president of the Alpine Club, that George was ultimately chosen to go on the reconnaissance mission. His selection would not last long: he 'failed' a cursory medical examination despite contrary evidence from tests at Oxford University that he was actually the fittest man on the expedition. While a 13-man team of climbers and scientists and soldiers left on the 4-month journey, George stayed in London, choosing to set aside his disappointment and concentrate on exploring the concept of using oxygen at altitude to counter the thin air at the top of Everest.

The reconnaissance mission would be a partial success. The mountain was reached and climbed to a point from where a camp could be established to launch an ascent allowing the area to be mapped for the first time. The team also returned with tales of a barren land, a behemoth of granite swept by blizzards and a collection of plant specimens. Mallory told a crowd of thousands who packed out a London theatre that he was prepared to try but had doubts that Everest could be climbed.

George would ultimately be included in the expedition in 1922, seconded not as the brilliant climber he was but as the man in charge of the oxygen apparatus he had not only designed himself but had built from experiments conducted in a steel tank at Oxford.

The new equipment, however, sparked a bitter debate over the use of oxygen in the climb and whether it would constitute an artificial boost and thereby be seen as a kind of 'cheating'. George argued that it was akin to improvements in boots, clothes, hats, tents, tools and nutrition, but the purists of the Alpine Club described it as a heresy and only grudgingly approved its inclusion.

By the time the team had arrived at the foot of Everest in May, the team leaders had decided against the use of oxygen – and George. Charles Bruce was the portly, ageing expedition leader and Colonel Edward Strutt its snobbish second in command. Strutt despised George, even condemning him for wearing his specially-made green jacket of balloon fabric stuffed with eiderdown – warmer than anything known at the time – while the others struggled in Norfolk tweed suits and layers of cotton, wool and silk.

As the approaching monsoon threatened to shut down the expedition, Strutt decided to make an attempt with four climbers but not allowing them oxygen. Mallory would lead with Howard Somervell, Edward Norton and Henry Morshead, leaving the only other recognised climber – George Finch – at base camp.

George had been laid low with dysentery but had expected two-man teams and was set to climb with Somervell who was one of the few who supported the use of oxygen. When George realised what had happened he chose two soldiers – a British officer named Geoffrey Bruce and a Gurkha named Tejbir to climb with him, despite the fact that neither had climbed a mountain before.

By the time Mallory and the others returned, frostbitten and dazed after two days on the mountain and being forced back at just under 27,000 feet, George and his novice team-mates had prepared and tested the oxygen equipment, substituting faulty breathing tubes with a makeshift mouthpiece made from toy football bladders he had bought from a market in India.

The three men set off in good spirits, the oxygen clearly making a physical and mental difference. All seemed possible as they moved steadily upwards, but within hours the weather had closed in, forcing them to seek shelter on the north-west ridge. Here, the men would spend almost 48-hours huddled in a tiny tent, anchored precariously to the side of the mountain as the winds threatened to lift their shelter and cast them into oblivion. On the second morning they emerged, determined to push for the top.

Tejbir lasted only a few-hundred-metres before collapsing, exhausted. He returned to the tent while George and Bruce continued upward, past the mark of Mallory and the others before altering their line and climbing across the face to shield themselves from the fierce winds. Once beneath the summit, George began climbing upwards once more until he heard a shout. Bruce had broken a glass valve, could get no air and was about to faint and fall to his death. George reached down and grabbed his companion by the shoulder hauling him back to safety on a tiny ledge. They were at 27,300 feet and could see the cairn of small rocks that crown the summit.

George shared his oxygen with Bruce while using a toolkit and spare parts to fit a replacement valve. The oxygen system was working again but Bruce could go no further. George thought momentarily about going on alone but quickly abandoned the attempt. Bruce would die without him. 'Turn back,' he called above the rising wind. Tears filled Bruce's eyes in response.

Although some would call it a heroic failure, the public responded to George Finch and George Mallory as returning heroes, filling town halls across Britain for months as they recounted their adventure. George Finch in particular held the halls spellbound as he used glass lantern slides taken from his photographs to illustrate the alien landscape and exotic cultures of a land beyond their imagination.

Although his success filled the coffers of the Everest Committee, Arthur Hinks could only seethe at the admiration of George, using his association with *The Times* newspaper to continue belittling his achievements. Against the advice of promoters, Hinks banned George from spruiking his achievements and refused to allow lectures in Europe, insisting wrongly it would impact negatively on the marketing of the expedition movie made by John Noel.

The row reached its peak in the summer of 1923 as the committee finalised the expedition members for the next assault on Everest. George challenged the right of Hinks to prevent him lecturing before attempting to find a compromise but Hinks would not relent and threatened his expulsion from the 1924 expedition. In his frustration, George accepted his fate calmly: 'I understand indirectly that for reasons doubtless sufficient to the committee I am not to be asked to join the next expedition, notwithstanding the relative success gained by my own party and my subsequent very willing services in connection with the improvements in the new oxygen apparatus.' Instead of using his scientific genius to build a better oxygen system and manage it on the mountain, the committee chose a 21-year-old, third year chemistry student, named Sandy Irvine who would not only oversee the oxygen but partner Mallory when they made their attempt on 8 June 1924 from which they would not return.

We will never really know but there are many historians and writers – including the novelist Jeffrey Archer whose 2009 novel *Paths of Glory* was based on the life of Mallory – who believe mountaineering history might have been very different if it had been the two Georges – Mallory and Finch – on Everest that day.

Did the belligerent interference of an arrogant administrator with no climbing experience cost the lives of two men and the chance of conquering the world's highest peak almost three decades before Edmund Hillary and Tenzig Norgay would do so?

Hillary was quick to credit George Finch when he triumphed on 29 May 1953 using a revamped version of George's oxygen equipment. Now aged 70 and living in India where India's first Prime Minister Jawaharlal Nehru had personally chosen him to manage the country's first scientific research facility, George and his third wife Agnes Johnston had reared three daughters in the years since his Everest disappointment.

He had made his last ascent in 1933 after a climbing holiday turned to tragedy, watching three friends ignore his advice and try to traverse a dangerous section of a mountainside before falling to their deaths. Although he was clearly blameless, the experience convinced him, at the age of just 51, to retreat to his other passion – science and teaching.

By then he had also established himself as one of Britain's most senior scientists, a professor at London's Imperial College, member of the Royal Society and the recipient of its highest honour, the Hughes Medal, which he was awarded at the height of World War II. George's work had helped in the scientific understanding of the behavior of fire and incendiary bombs and helped London's defence strategies during the blitz by improving fire fighting techniques. He was also instrumental in the design of a range of bombs, including the famous J-Bomb, that created havoc across German cities during the retaliations of 1944 and 1945.

There would be some reckoning in his later years when, in 1959, he was elected president of the Alpine Club. But even with this official vindication, it is difficult not to wonder what might have been, had George Finch and George Mallory climbed together in 1924.

✄ Robert Wainwright is a London-based freelance journalist and author with more than thirty years experience in national daily newspapers. He has won a number of journalism awards over the years, the most notable being as a three-time finalist with Australia's most prestigious journalism prize, the Walkley Awards, in 2004, 2009 and 2010. His career as an author grew from his journalism and he has written and had published nine non-fiction titles, ranging from crime and mystery to biographies and social history. Two of the books have been finalists in prominent Australian literary awards. One has been turned into a television movie, another was the basis for a musical and two others are currently in production as feature films.

JESSICA MITFORD AND THE RED SCARE

Words by Terence Towles Canote

Jessica Mitford was known as the 'red sheep' of the Mitford sisters. She was only 15 when she became an adherent of Communism. And while her political leanings would at times cause some difficulties with her family (whose politics ran the gamut from Diana's fascism to Nancy's moderate socialism), any difficulties her political beliefs might have caused with her family were nothing compared to the problems they sometimes caused with what would become her adopted country, the United States. Indeed, the United States would enter the period known as the Red Scare following World War II, a period of heightened concern over Communist influence in the nation.

It was in 1939 that Jessica and her husband Esmond Romilly (Winston Churchill's nephew-by-marriage) migrated to the United States. It was not long after their arrival that Jessica attracted the interest of the Federal Bureau of Investigation (FBI). Curiously, the earliest documents in the FBI's file on Jessica deal as much with her sister Unity as they do Jessica. In fact, the very first document in the file is an International News Service article on Unity's friendship with Adolph Hitler bearing the rather sensationalistic headline 'Her Heart Crushed by Hitler's Fist'. Here it must be pointed out that the FBI apparently never suspected Jessica of sharing Unity's political beliefs. A memo from 16 June 1942 notes an interview with an Englishwoman, who had been living the United States for 8 years and claimed to know the Mitfords. In the interview the woman said that Jessica had broken with her family when she married Esmond and had never returned because of her family's 'pro-Nazi attitude'.

With the outbreak of World War II, Esmond joined the Royal Canadian Air Force. Sadly, in 1941 his plane was shot down over the North Sea and Esmond was considered missing in action.

During World War II Jessica worked for the Office of Price Administration (OPA), a Federal agency in charge of price controls during World War II. Of course, this meant that she had to undergo a background check when she applied. Jessica passed the background check, although the FBI appears to have had some awareness at the time of her political leanings. A document in her FBI file from 18 March 1943 states: 'Associates of applicant advised she talked fluently in favour of Communist ideals at that time but has since become more conservative.' The document goes on to say: 'Character and morale of applicant good. Loyalty to allied cause unquestioned.'

It was while she was working for the Office of Price Administration that Jessica met attorney Robert Treuhaft, known as Bob, who worked in the OPA's legal department. Jessica was eventually transferred to the San Francisco office of the OPA and Bob transferred to San Francisco not long after. The two were married in Santa Rosa, California in 1943. Among other things the two shared the same politics. In 1944, Jessica not only became a naturalised citizen of the United States, but also a member of the Communist Party.

Jessica's activities with the Communist Party did not go unnoticed by the FBI. In a document dated 25 January 1945 it is noted that she was '...an active member of the Communist Political Association in San Francisco, California...' and '...previously had been active in the Communist Party.' The FBI would maintain an interest in Jessica for decades afterwards. Of the FBI's constant surveillance she once said: 'We were under eternal vigilance. By that time, I took it casually. The children would cry out, "Mother, milkman's here." "Mother, laundryman's here." "Mother, FBI's here."' Indeed, while the earliest documents in Jessica's FBI file date to 1940, the latest documents date to the '70s.

That the FBI would keep Jessica under heavy surveillance starting in 1945 should come as no surprise, as the end of World War II would also mark the beginning of the era of the Red Scare in the United States. Communist influence had actually been of some concern for some time to the United States government. In fact, the Red Scare of the late '40s and early '50s is more properly termed 'the Second Red Scare', the first having taken place in the wake of the Bolshevik Russian Revolution of 1917 and lasting until about 1920. The first incarnation of the House of Un-American Activities Committee (HUAC) was established in 1938. HUAC was an investigative committee of the United States House of Representatives whose purpose was to investigate alleged subversive activities. Initially it was meant to look into possible Nazi ties in the U.S., although it would turn its eyes to Communists soon enough. In 1938 HUAC investigated charges that the Federal Theatre Project had been overrun by Communists. In 1939 they investigated the American Youth Congress for some of its leaders' alleged ties to Communism.

It was in 1945 that the House Un-American Activities Committee became a standing committee of the House of Representatives. It would make headlines in 1947 when it investigated alleged Communist influence in Hollywood, an investigation that would result in ten screenwriters and directors being cited for contempt of Congress (the 'Hollywood Ten'). The investigation would also mark the beginning of the Hollywood blacklist, whereby entertainers could be denied employment if they were even suspected of Communist beliefs or sympathies.

The state of California had its own equivalent to the House of Un-American Activities Committee. The California Senate Factfinding Subcommittee on Un-American Activities (SUAC) was a subcommittee of the Standing Rules Committee of the California State Senate. Like HUAC it was meant to investigate alleged subversive activity. It was established in 1941.

Given Jessica Mitford and Robert Treuhaft's political beliefs, it should come as no surprise that in 1951 the California Senate Factfinding Subcommittee on Un-American Activities subpoenaed Jessica and Bob. The subpoenas were issued specifically due to their involvement with the East Bay Civil Rights Congress, an organisation launched by the Communist Party to fight racism in Oakland, Berkeley, and Richmond, California. As might be expected, Jessica was asked such questions as 'Have you been the director of the East Bay Civil Rights Congress since May 1950?', 'Do you maintain a bank account for the East Bay Civil Rights Congress in the Wells Fargo Bank?', and 'Is your husband, Robert Treuhaft, legal counsel for the Civil Rights Congress?' Jessica was also asked the question always asked at SUAC and HUAC hearings, 'Have you now or have you ever been a member of the Communist Party?' To each of the questions she pleaded the Fifth Amendment (under which one does not have to answer questions which might incriminate himself or herself). For reasons that are not known to this day, Jessica was then asked, 'Are you a member of the Berkeley Tennis Club?' Thinking she had been asked if she was a member of the Berkeley Tenants Club, a union for renters, Jessica once more pleaded the Fifth Amendment. Laughter filled the Senate chamber, although the subcommittee itself was not amused. They dismissed Jessica as an uncooperative witness. Neither Jessica nor Bob were charged with contempt, although for a time Jessica thought they might be. In a letter to her mother, she wrote: 'We haven't been cited yet for contempt, so maybe they will forget about it...'

In 1953 both Jessica Mitford and Bob were called before the House of Un-American Activities Committee. In his testimony before HUAC, Bob made his disapproval of the proceedings clear and even quoted President Harry Truman (who had not been out of office that long) by saying of McCarthyism: 'It is the spread of fear and the destruction of faith at every level of our society. This horrible cancer is eating at the vitals of America, and it can destroy the great edifice of freedom.' Both Bob and Jessica refused to cooperate with HUAC and pleaded the Fifth Amendment. Sadly, in a letter to her mother, Jessica pointed out the toll that the HUAC hearings had on many who appeared before them. People ranging from school teachers to waitresses to carpenters lost their jobs because they had simply been called to testify before the committee.

The year 1954 marked the beginning of the end for the Second Red Scare in the United States. It was the year that Senator Joe McCarthy of Wisconsin (who had given his name to the term 'McCarthyism') was largely discredited during what became known as the Army-McCarthy hearings. While Senator McCarthy was actually a latecomer to the Communist witch hunts, he had become the politician most associated with them. Various Supreme Court decisions would also play a role in the end of the Red Scare. In 1956 in the case of Slochower v. Board of Education the Court ruled that a New York City professor could not be fired because he pled the Fifth Amendment when asked if he had been a member of the Communist Party. In the 1957 case Yates v. United States the Supreme Court overturned the convictions of 14 Communists. That same year, in the case Watkins v. United States, the Supreme Court restricted Congress's powers to conduct investigations, including the ability to cite people in contempt of Congress. It was a serious blow to the House of Un-American Activities Committee and the sort of tactics they had used for years.

As for Jessica and Bob, they left the Communist Party in 1958 after Nikita Khrushchev revealed Stalin's atrocities as the head of the U.S.S.R. The two continued to support liberal and leftist causes, remaining active in the Civil Rights Movement and the Free Speech Movement in Berkeley, California.

While the Red Scare crawled to a halt in the mid-Fifties, its reverberations were still being felt in the Sixties and Seventies. And while the Treuhafts had left the Communist Party in 1958, Jessica's association with the Party would often be brought up when she was mentioned. To wit, when her exposé on the American funeral industry *The American Way of Death* was published in 1963, undertakers in the United States went on the attack by trying to portray Jessica and her book as downright un-American. They brought up her former membership in the Communist Party, her testimony before the House of Un-American Activities Committee, and her association with the Civil Rights Congress.

Undertakers weren't the only ones attacking Jessica as un-American because of *The American Way of Death*. Representative James B. Utt, a right-wing Congressman from California, denounced her in the *Congressional Record*. He pointed out that she was the wife of Robert Treuhaft, who had twice been identified as a Communist in the seventh report of the California Senate Factfinding Subcommittee on Un-American Activities and that both of them had pled the Fifth Amendment when testifying before the subcommittee. He pointed out she was once the financial director of the California Labour School (an educational house alleged by conservatives to have Communist ties). He pointed out that she had been director of the Civil Rights Congress. Utt even said that profits from *The American Way of Death* '... no doubt will find their way into coffers of the Communist Party U.SA'. As to the man making such accusations, Utt voted against the Civil Rights Act of 1960, and would vote against the Civil Rights Act of 1964 and the Civil Rights Act of 1968. He would also vote against the Voting Rights Act of 1965.

As mentioned earlier, reverberations from the Second Red Scare in the United States were being felt as late as the Seventies. It was in 1973 that Jessica was hired by San Jose State University as a Distinguished Professor of Sociology during the fall semester, a high honour for someone who had never attended school, let alone university. Unfortunately, Jessica arrived at San Jose State University to not only find copies of the school paper and assorted announcements waiting for her, but a note for her to report to personnel to take a loyalty oath and be fingerprinted. As might be expected, she threw the note in the waste basket.

Unfortunately, San Jose State University insisted that Jessica must take the loyalty oath and be fingerprinted, something which she refused to do. In response, the university's administration fired her. For many professors this would have been the end of the affair, but not for Jessica. She continued to teach her classes, even though she was not paid for them, and took San Jose State University to court over the matter of the loyalty oath and fingerprinting. Throughout the ordeal she received overwhelming support from her students. The university's sociology department supported her and defied the administration's order to find a replacement for her. The *Spartan Daily*, the university's student newspaper, even denounced the administration in an editorial, as did the *San Francisco Chronicle*.

Jessica eventually gave in and signed the loyalty oath. San Jose State University reinstated her as a professor. The university also paid her, although they withheld her September pay-cheque as she did not sign her loyalty oath until October 1. She continued to fight the fingerprint requirement. In the end the court ruled that the fingerprint requirement was not supported under any law.

The Red Scare of the late Forties and early Fifties was a time when many lives were ruined. People lost their jobs. Some even committed suicide. Jessica, who had actually been a Communist, weathered the storm, even though she had to endure a good deal of harassment to do so. As the 1970s progressed and the Red Scare receded into memory, she continued her career as a muckraking journalist and wrote several more books. When she died from lung cancer at age 78 in 1996 she was remembered in newspaper obituaries as a muckraking journalist, a clever polemicist, and, particularly in the United States, the author of *The American Way of Death*. While it was acknowledged she had been a Communist, she was not condemned for it. One can only suspect her detractors during the Red Scare were very unhappy.

Terence Towles Canote is the author of the book *Television: Rare and Well Done*. He runs the blog A Shroud of Thoughts. He has been published in *Capper's Weekly*, *The Old Cowboy Picture Show*, and other small press publications.

THE GRIT IN THE PEARL

THE LIFE OF MARGARET WHIGHAM

Words by Lyndsy Spence

She was always a headstrong woman, always used to getting her own way. This character trait, or flaw (depending if one were a friend or a foe), was apparent in girlhood. Born Ethel Margaret Whigman in 1912 in Newton Mearns near Glasgow, she dropped her parents' choice of Ethel and insisted on being known as Margaret. Margaret was the only child of Helen and George Whigham. Her father, a shrewd businessman from Prestwick was a self-made millionaire and chairman of the Celanese Corporation; and her mother – perhaps knowing where to hit Margaret where it would hurt – threatened her with a sibling if she misbehaved. A beautiful child with a nervous stutter, she was petted and spoiled and protected, but it was a misplaced love, and early on the die was cast.

Perhaps the earliest and most vivid example of Margaret's character lies in an anecdote from her adolescence. She had been a pupil at a progressive Hewitt school in New York City (where she lived until the age of 14) run by an Englishwoman, and although she realised that she needed little formal education, after all daddy's millions would cushion the pinpricks of every day life, she took an interest in history. Obediently completing her homework – a history project on the Medieval period – she cut illustrations from an old and valuable library book and pasted them into her jotter. The project was submitted and hell broke loose. But Margaret did not understand what the fuss was about: she had simple done what was asked of her. This blind spot remained with her, always.

When Margaret was brought to England the storm clouds were already forming. In 1928, at the age of 15, she was seduced by the future actor David Niven during a holiday in Bembridge on the Isle of Wight. To the fury of her father and the shame of her mother, Margaret became pregnant and was whisked off to a London clinic for a secret termination. She continued to adore David Niven until the day he died and was among the VIP guests at his memorial service in London.

Not a hint of scandal broke, and Margaret was sent to finishing school in Paris. In many ways, she was already finished, and she returned to London to a frivolous existence of parties and balls. In 1930 she was presented at Court and was named Debutante of the Year. Her striking face was photographed for society magazines and she peered out of *Tatler, The Lady* and *The Sketch*, lantern-jawed, her grey-blue eyes fixed in a cold stare, and her dark brown hair neatly waved around her face. She looked back with affection on those years, calling them 'heaven' with 'three parties every night and not a care in the world'. As the economic depression of the early 1930s unravelled around her, Margaret developed something of a social conscience. The *Daily Express* reported:

> As an example to the girlhood of Britain, the lovely Margaret Whigham has decided, in the interests of economy, to have her hair re-set only once a fortnight in future, and to stop wearing stockings in the evening. On the other hand, to stimulate trade, she has just bought four new evening dresses.

The socialist publication, the *Daily Worker,* viewed it as far from charitable and they wrote: 'This should be a lesson to the wives of the unemployed, whose extravagant habits include setting their hair in curl-papers every day and buying no dresses at all.'

Margaret meant well, but her sentiments were poorly executed. This is best displayed in her memoirs, when she recalled the war-time necessity of the evacuation of her children to Lord and Lady Aberconway in North Wales. She divulged that 'Christabel Aberconway had decided to take the children of her friends as paying guests at 10 pounds a head in preference to having the Liverpool evacuees forced upon her'.

However, before the war came and spoiled Margaret's fun (or did it?) she was a celebrated girl about town. She was briefly engaged to Lord Beaverbrook's son, Max Aitken, and then to Charles Guy Fulke Greville, the 7th Earl of Warwick. Feeling that she was not sufficiently in love, she ditched her suitors in favour of Charles Sweeney. In February 1933, after converting to the Roman Catholic faith, she married Sweeney, a dashing American golfer and businessman. It was heralded as the society wedding of the year, with the press and public surrounding Brompton Oratory for a glance of the much-publicised Norman Hartnell wedding dress with its 28-by-9-feet train, causing the traffic in Kensington to come to a standstill. It was said by Margaret that Princess Elizabeth copied the design for her wedding to Prince Philip in November 1947.

Margaret had three children with Sweeney: a daughter, who was stillborn at 8-months in 1933; another daughter Frances born in 1937 (she later married Charles Manners, 10th Duke of Rutland); and a son, Brian, born in 1940. Margaret also had 8 miscarriages during the course of their marriage. While she recuperated, Sweeney would visit her after work before dressing and going out for the evening, leaving her at home feeling miserable and increasingly insecure. Although distressed by her husband's infidelities, something he did not hide from her, she adored him and they would remain friends long after their divorce.

In 1934, it seemed Margaret had the world at her feet. P.G. Wodehouse referenced her in his Anglicised version of Cole Porter's song 'You're the Top' from the musical *Anything Goes*. He replaced Porter's original lyric 'You're an O'Neill drama, You're Whistler's mama' with 'You're Mussolini, You're Mrs Sweeney'. She continued to live a gilded life until, in 1943, she suffered a near fatal fall down a lift shaft while visiting her chiropodist on Bond Street. She later recalled:

> I fell 40-feet to the bottom of the lift shaft. The only thing that saved me was the lift cable, which broke my fall. I must have clutched at it, for it was later found that all my finger nails were torn off. I apparently fell on to my knees and cracked the back of my head against the wall.

After her recovery, Margaret's friends noted that not only had she lost all sense of taste and smell due to nerve damage, she also had become sexually voracious. 'Go to bed early and often,' she was apt to say.

Margaret and Sweeney divorced in 1947. She had romances with several men including a brief engagement to a Texan-born banker, Joseph Thomas, of Lehman Brothers, which ended after he fell in love with another woman. There was also Theodore 'Ted' Rousseau, curator of the Metropolitan Museum of Art, who was, she recalled, 'highly intelligent, witty and self-confident to the point of arrogance'. That relationship ended because Margaret feared Ted was not stepfather material.

In 1950, she met Ian Campbell, the 11th Duke of Argyll, who was married to his second wife Louise, whose nickname was 'Oui Oui', but Margaret referred to her as 'wee-wee'. Margaret and the duke, known as 'Big Ian', met on the luxurious Golden Arrow boat-train which operated Channel crossing between London and Paris. As they began to converse, Ian confessed that he had seen Margaret descending the staircase at the Cafe de Paris and ungallantly turned to his wife and said he had just seen 'the girl he would marry someday'. They were to meet again, by chance, at Claridges upon which Margaret told Ian she was 'a man short' for a luncheon party she was giving the following day. He stepped in to make up the numbers.

The two soon began to confide in one another, and Ian disclosed to Margaret his marital woes, increasing debts and his inability to restore the Argyll family seat, Inveraray Castle. She later wrote:

> Ian was obviously lonely, and depressed by the burden of debt and mismanagement that he had inherited from his elderly cousin, the 10th Duke. I was also alone, and felt drawn towards this troubled man who had so much charm. According to my diary, on March 25 1950, we spent the entire day together, having lunch in the country at an old mill house, dining at Maxim's that evening, and going on afterwards to the Lido.

Ten days later Ian proposed to Margaret on the condition that they would marry when he was free from Louise. She readily accepted and they were married on 23 March 1951. Margaret's friends and ex-husband warned her against marrying Ian, who had a reputation for being a fortune hunter, a heavy drinker, a gambler, and for beating his former wives. His first wife, Janet Aitken, the daughter of Lord Beaverbrook, was 17 when she married him and during their honeymoon his true character emerged when he shook her violently and told her to 'stop snivelling'. During their ill-fated honeymoon he also took Janet to a Parisian bordello as she 'had a lot to learn'. Later, on a cruise to Jamaica, Janet discovered he had stolen her jewels to pay his gambling debts. She realised he had married her for her money.

Margaret's ex-husband, Charles Sweeney, also attempted to warn her of the folly she was committing, when he wrote:

> I'll never forget you or love anyone else. I know that now and I also know that nothing I can
> say or do will change your mind. Therefore . . I do wish you luck and I hope you'll be happy.
> I only hope you're not deluding yourself that Campbell is inspired by any great love, because
> he's not. He couldn't be and you'll be making your crowning mistake if you think anything
> else. He married his first two wives for money and you're no exception.

Furthermore, a mutual friend of both Margaret and Ian warned her that Ian had said: 'Now I'll get all my bills paid.' When Margaret later took offence at him for saying that he 'only married rich women', it was not because of the content of his statement, but because he had said it in front of the servants.

Knowing that his beloved Margaret desperately wanted to become the Duchess of Argyll, George Whigham insisted that Ian sign a Deed of Gift which listed certain valuable items as security for the money he had laid out. Margaret had asked her father to fund a new roof for Inveraray Castle because Ian threatened to have it removed to avoid paying the rates bill. The document was regarded as superfluous, but Ian signed it anyway. Little did Margaret or her father know that Ian harboured a spiteful surprise which would be exposed when their marriage was dragged through the divorce court a decade later.

Ian himself had not been near the castle in 20 years, and to meet the death duties of the previous duke, the trustees of his estate sold the Island of Tiree. Margaret financed Ian's latest scheme when he decided to exhume the wreck of the Spanish ship the *Duque de Florencia* in Tobermory Bay on the Island of Mull, which he claimed would net him £30-million. Margaret not only paid for the investigation of the wreck, but also the bill the Royal Navy sent him for its assistance in the project. Later she would also complain that she had had to pay for Ian's children's school fees. Yet, in spite of Margaret and her father's generosity, Ian demanded she give up her London flat. Already discord had set in.

During their first year of marriage, Margaret sensed the flaws in her husband's personality. He had attempted to humiliate her at his daughter Lady Jeanne's coming out ball by dancing with is first wife, Janet, and ignoring Margaret.

And, on holiday in Kingston, Jamaica, he had tried to beat her up and she was saved from assault when her friends intervened. He further displayed a sadistic and unpredictable streak when, on their way to a celebratory dinner at the French Embassy on Coronation Day in June 1953, he suddenly jumped out of the car and told her she could go herself. He was enraged when Margaret decided to do just that, and he went off to his London club, White's.

Assuming her husband was content with an open marriage, Margaret began to invite her male friends to the castle, but one member on the guest list was a step too far for Ian. The guest was the German diplomat Sigismund von Braun, a noted anti-Nazi, and whose brother invented the V-2 rocket. But Ian, a former prisoner of war in a German camp for 5 years, was troubled by the intrusion. Margaret had, in many ways, played into Ian's hands.

Having been divorced by his first two wives, Ian would be the one to do the divorcing this time. Although they had been living separately for years, Ian was determined to expose Margaret as an adulteress. For his plan to render successful he would need evidence, and a ruthless man in the grand scheme of things, he did not shirk from setting his wife up. He took advantage of Margaret being out of the country and entered her house on Upper Grosvenor Street where he stole diaries, letters and photographs. When he returned to locate a missing diary for 1956-59 he brought him with his daughter, Lady Jeanne. This time Margaret was at home, and as she turned out her bedroom light she saw two figures entering her bedroom. She later recalled:

> I immediately began dialing 999, but Ian pinioned my arms to prevent this, while Jeanne snatched up my diary. After this they made a rapid exit. It was a horrible experience, and the next day I suffered from delayed shock.

Margaret sued Lady Jeanne for trespass, which was settled out of court. She would have sued Ian, too, except by law he had a right to enter her home as they were still married. Unhappy with the British legal system, Margaret fought against the stolen items being used in evidence and she took her case to the House of Lords before the issue was referred back to the Court of Session in Edinburgh, where the case was to be heard. In a bid to destroy Margaret, Ian attempted to have her certified insane by arranging for his doctor to draw up the necessary committal papers. However, he had to obtain a second signature and the latter doctor refused and warned Margaret what her husband was plotting.

The hearing for evidence began on 26 February 1963. The judge, Lord Wheatley, was said to have influenced his jury to revolt against Margaret when it came to their verdict. He was a teetotal, Jesuit-educated Catholic, and such was his background, he was shocked by Margaret's behaviour. He was also a Campbell on his mother's side.

The first witness admitted to the court was Ian, and the first legal objection arose early when reference was made to one of the diaries he had stolen from Upper Grosvenor Street, but Lord Wheatley permitted the evidence to be used. Ian was also given preferential treatment when, due to an alleged medical difficulty, he remained seated whilst giving evidence, whereas Margaret had to stand for 13 hours. Ian said the marriage had been happy up until 1954, after which date Margaret's social life posed a threat to their domesticity, and she stayed out as late as 4am. This behaviour, he said, caused arguments between them. Speaking of the night he and his daughter had broken into Margaret's house and used restraint on her, Ian explained he had noticed the diary under a telephone which Margaret had picked up, and having found it, he and Jeanne departed. The reason Jeanne accompanied him, he said, was to protect him from being accused by Margaret of 'jumping into bed together'.

Damning evidence was produced, which would ultimately seal Margaret's fate. Ian produced a collection of Polaroids which came to be known as 'the headless man'. They showed Margaret, nude save for her signature three-strand pearl necklace, with a gentleman whose back was turned to the camera. She would not disclose who he was (she never did) and a list of over 80 possible names were drawn up. It was believed the man was either Douglas Fairbanks, Jnr. or Winston Churchill's son-in-law, Duncan Sandys, Minister of Defence. Indeed, Margaret admitted that 'the only Polaroid camera in the country at that time had been lent to the Ministry of Defence'. In recent times the headless man was revealed as William H. 'Bill' Lyons, then sales director of Pan American World Airways. The judge proclaimed Margaret to be 'a highly sexed woman who had ceased to be satisfied with normal sexual relations' and had started to indulge in what he could only describe as 'disgusting sexual activities to gratify a debased sexual appetite'.

When the divorce case came to a conclusion in May 1963, Margaret was at the Ritz Hotel in Paris with her married lover. In her 1975 memoir, *Forget Not*, she wrote:

> As soon as I reached my room I put through a call to my solicitor in Edinburgh. 'It couldn't be much worse,' he told me. 'I've never in my life heard such a cruel judgement.' He went on to repeat some of the things the judge, Lord Wheatley, had said about me. As he spoke, I knew I was listening to my world disintegrate. The words I was hearing constituted nothing less than a savage character assassination. I could scarcely believe that any man – let alone a judge – could be so merciless or capable of inflicting such unnecessary pain on another human being.

Ian was granted his divorce, and Margaret had become a social pariah. The media circus, the speculation over the Polaroids, and the exposure of her behaviour conspired to destroy her reputation. Furthermore, she became estranged from her children who were appalled at their mother. Ian was prepared to cash in on the spectacle, and he sold his story to *People*. Before the article was published in November 1964, Margaret applied for an injunction to stop the printing of her private letters. Nevertheless, the first installment was published, but her solicitor prevented the publication of any more after it had come to Margaret's attention that Ian wanted to make public her medical files detailing her physical and psychological health. The judge agreed with Margaret, and this became known as the 'Argyll law'.

But Margaret was to have the last laugh. After humiliating her in the pages of *People*, Ian was asked to resign from White's, his beloved London club, or risk being thrown out. With a heavy heart he chose the former. It was Margaret's first husband, Charles Sweeney, who had used his influence at the club to have Ian expelled. With a certain amount of glee, she said: 'Though the mills of God grind slowly, yet they grind exceedingly small.'

Margaret died in 1993 at the age of 80, having spent the evening of her life at St George's nursing home in Pimlico. In her later years she found herself impoverished after investing in several, ill-advised schemes. She did, however, maintain her standards. When luncheon was served at midday in the nursing home she refused to eat it. Only servants ate their meal at 12, she said, and she defiantly waited until 1 o'clock. Though the food was cold, Margaret could, at least, take satisfaction in knowing she had the last word.

SOMETHING HIGHER THAN A FRIEND

Words by Lyndsy Spence

Diana was 14-years-old when she first met James Lees-Milne, known to his friends as 'Jim'. He had come down to Asthall Manor, the family home in Oxfordshire that was said to be haunted by a poltergeist, with Tom Mitford in the summer of 1924.

Both Diana and Jim were intrigued by one another, and he was bewitched by her beauty as he silently observed her sitting next to Tom as he played the piano. Diana, too, thought Jim the cleverest person she had met. She was impressed by his loathing of games and his preference for sitting indoors, listening to classical music and conversing about art and literature. Tom appeared to share an easy-going, brotherly type of affection with Jim, but their schoolboy camaraderie concealed a discreet affair that had taken place at Eton. The close bond between Diana and Tom reminded Jim of his loneliness and lack of familial ties – he despised his father, saw little of his mother, and had nothing in common with his siblings. Adding to his misery, all through his childhood and early adolescent years, Jim wished he were a girl. Society's expectations placed on Jim as a boy, and his countrified father's disapproval, conspired to make him 'feel desperately ashamed' of his wish. Adding to Jim's feelings of shame was the guilt of his affair with Tom, and he desired to replace him with Diana, a socially acceptable catalyst for romance.

After Jim departed Asthall, he immediately wrote Diana a letter, asking her: 'May I treat you as a much cherished sister to whom I can say everything? You don't realise how essential they are to boys. Why are you so amazingly sympathique as well as charming?' Diana, who was surrounded by six sisters and an all-female staff, was unsure how to respond to such flattery. She acted with indifference, which could have been mistaken as modesty – an appealing attribute in one so beautiful.

Jim returned to Asthall, and he, Tom and Diana became a peculiar trio. When the other Mitford children were outside riding and hunting, they spent their days indoors, lapping up joyous hours in the library where Jim expressed his devotion by teaching Diana to read the classics. They read poetry and fantasised about going to live in Greece, where they 'would scorn material things and live on a handful of grapes by the sea'. Around this period, Jim had appointed himself as Diana's faithful correspondent and the letters exchanged during this precarious time provide an insight into her outlook. As her intellect developed, she felt comfortable to confide her innermost thoughts to Jim. She told him: 'There will never be another Shelley. I wish I had been alive then to marry him. He was more beautiful physically and mentally than an angel.' And her philosophy on life was extremely modern for a sheltered teenager in the 1920s: 'Why on earth should two souls (I wish there was a better word, I think SPIRIT is better). Why on earth should two spirits who are in love a bit have to marry … and renounce all other men and women?' Monogamy, to Diana, was 'SUPREMELY foolish', but she was quick to acknowledge that speaking of 'free love is almost a sin'. However, to dispel any hint of romance, she quickly informed Jim of his platonic place in her life: 'I sometimes feel that I love you too much, but you are my spiritual brother.'

In 1926, Diana left for Paris to spend a year studying art at the Cours Fénelon, and during this period her letters to Jim became few and far between. She had fallen in love with the city, and had formed a circle of admirers who were a world away from Jim and his shy advances disguised by the written word. The ageing artist Paul César Helleu feted Diana, and this form of flattery coming from an adult turned her head more than Jim's romantic prose.

After Diana's departure for Paris, Jim had become morbidly obsessed with a recent divorcee, Joanie, the daughter of his mother's cousin. Jim sent her love poetry – the typical gesture he would use time and time again with those he admired – and Joanie responded by driving down to Eton to take him to tea. In the New Year of 1926, they eventually began an affair, resulting in Joanie becoming pregnant. However, there is no certainty that Jim fathered the child, for she had so many casual affairs. The baby was stillborn, and Jim was haunted by guilt, stemming from his view that he had caused a human life, conceived in sin, to perish. Deeply disturbed by the incident, Jim fled England for Grenoble, where he studied a university course in French. His thoughts turned to Diana and the memories he held from their happier days in the library at Asthall Manor. The notion of being in love with an unworldly teenager was less troublesome than his love affair with the older Joanie, whose life came to a tragic end when she drowned herself at Monte Carlo.

Overwhelmed by a sense of nostalgia, Jim wrote to Diana, in which he played to her frivolous vanity by addressing her as 'Mona' (after the Mona Lisa). Her letter, after a spell of silence, 'dropped here today like the gentle dew from heaven. I cannot express my delight but imagine it as being intense … How I would adore to have a picture of you by M. Helleu'. He implored Diana to send him a memento; a snapshot of her Parisian self so he could see for himself if she had retained her Raphael face. 'You can't imagine what a joy it is to me the thought of having your face with me.' Diana had become accustomed to receiving compliments on her beauty, rather than her brains, and the tokens dispelled in his letters were not a rarity. Jim confessed: 'One can never love a friend too much,' though by now he thought of Diana as something 'higher than a friend'.

As for Diana, she was secretly pleased with Jim's infatuation and had begun to recognise her power over the opposite sex, using it to exploit those who cared about her. Her letters adopted a priggish tone, boasting of her liaisons with French boys, after which, she warned Jim: 'Don't feel jealous'. It thrilled her to evoke feelings of jealousy, to torment the poor love-sick Jim, and she made it clear that she only confided in him because he was 'so far from England's green and pleasant land, where scandal travels fast'.

The hedonistic atmosphere was not to last and Diana suffered a bitter blow when Helleu died, suddenly, of peritonitis. The man she worshipped, and who for 3 months had worshipped her, was dead. She turned to Jim for comfort. 'I shall never see him again …' her letter ached with melancholy '... never hear his voice saying, "Sweetheart, comme tu es belle."' In another letter, she confessed: 'Nobody will admire me again as he did.' Jim might have disagreed, but he refrained from telling her otherwise, and wrote only to comfort her.

When Diana returned to England for the Easter holidays she was disheartened by the family's new home, Swinbrook House – a grey, rectangular building designed by her father and decorated in mock rustic charm. Perhaps longing for a sense of familiarity, she wrote to Jim. 'I have grown a little older, and more intense in my passions of love, sorrow and worship of beauty. To look at, I am the same. Pray for me, to your gods whatever they are. I am very unhappy.' But, somewhere beneath her morbid facade, Diana was still a romantic at heart.

Jim's letters from that time, although an escape from the dullness of everyday life, drew her attention to his love for her. In a sophisticated manner, she declared: 'Sex is after all so unimportant in life. Beauty and art are what matter. Older people do not see my point of view.' Diana failed to elaborate on the 'older people', surely a jibe at Jim, who was 2 years her senior. She did not, however, discourage the correspondence. In a similar light as Helleu, Jim praised her looks. 'I have got dark skin and light hair and eyes which is an unattractive paradox,' she dismissed his compliment. In the same sentence, Diana asked if he had seen the various beauties: Mary Thynne, Lettice Lygon and Georgie Curzon, to name a few. Jim's passion could not be quelled, and Diana accepted his gifts of books, though she often critiqued his poetry when he sent it.

Finally, Jim was reunited with Diana in person. The sight of her in the flesh stunned him at first. She was no longer the sweet natured 14-year-old girl he had mentored in the library at Asthall. The long hair, which he had admired and likened to Botticelli's *Seaborne Venus*, had been cut short. Although not outwardly fashionable, she began to alter her looks to appear more grown-up in her appearance. This adult version of Diana inspired the same feelings of passion he had felt for Joanie, who wore chic clothes and Parisian scent.

Hoping to instigate a romance with Diana, though from afar, Jim impulsively sent her a poem. Diana's response was not what he had anticipated, and with a critical eye she advised him: 'Read Alice Meynell's short essay on false impressionism called *The Point of Honour*. This is not meant to be rude …' Adopting an intellectual tone, she confidently told him: 'Byron was a selfish, beautiful genius and not really more selfish than many men and most artists. As to Augusta, she was of the same temperament as I am, and just about as silly.'

Diana's letters to Jim fizzled out, and tormented by her lack of communication, he turned his attention to Diana's cousin and friend, Diana Churchill, whom he had met that summer. The other Diana, 'like a fairy' with her puny frame, pale complexion and red hair, was a haphazard substitute for his original love interest. In September, Diana invited him to the Churchill family home, Chartwell, and he readily accepted once he learned that Diana Mitford would also be staying with her brother, Tom. Unlike at Asthall and Swinbrook, where Jim could escape with Diana and Tom, the 'brats' (a Churchillian term of endearment) congregated in the drawing room and at the dining table. They listened to Winston Churchill's monologue on the Battle of Jutland as he shifted decanters and wine glasses, in place of the ships, around the table, furiously puffing on his cigar to represent the gun smoke. With Churchill's attention fixed on the children, his boisterous son Randolph seized an opportunity to flatter Diana, with whom he was madly in love. 'Papa,' he mischievously asked his father, 'guess who is older, our Diana or Diana M?'

'Our Diana,' came the reply from Churchill, spoiling Randolph's plan.

'Oh, Papa, nobody else thinks so but you!'

During the stay, Diana was surrounded by her two most ardent admirers and Jim noticed that she outwardly relished being in Randolph's company, despite her frequent protests about his immature behaviour. Jim could only look on, his hopes and feelings deflated.

In the new year of 1928, Jim returned to Swinbrook to stay for the weekend. Diana hoped to corner him for a congenial chat about literature, but the pleasant visit took a turn for the worse when, over dinner, Nancy praised an anti-German film she had watched at the cinema. Still harbouring a strong dislike for Germans, their father, Lord Redesdale, made his usual offensive remark: 'The only good German is a dead German.'

Leaping to the defence of the film and of the German people, Jim said: 'Anyhow, talking of atrocities, the worst in the whole war were committed by the Australians.'

'Be quiet and don't talk about what you don't understand. Young swine!' Lord Redesdale exploded.

Mortified by her father's outburst, Diana broke the heavy silence when she haughtily announced: 'I wish people needn't be so rude to their guests!'

Flexing his authority as master of the household, Lord Redesdale ordered Jim from Swinbrook. Frogmarched to the front door, he was thrown outside where it was teeming with rain. After several failed attempts to start up his motorcycle, he sneaked back into the house and crept up to bed.

Awaking at 6 o'clock the next morning, Jim bumped into Lord Redesdale, stalking the hallway, as he did every morning, wearing his paisley print robe and drinking tea from a thermos. Anticipating another scene, Jim was pleasantly surprised when Lord Redesdale appeared to have forgotten the offensive exchange and greeted him warmly.

The turbulent visit settled into a bittersweet memory for Jim and, although he did not know it at the time, it would be his last visit with Diana at Swinbrook. He rightly sensed that Diana's mind was focused on finding a suitable husband to rescue her from the great boredom of family life. With his 'impecunious and melancholic' nature, Jim knew he was not an ideal candidate, and long after he had departed from her life, Diana remained 'the unattainable object of his desire'.

In 1928, Diana met and became engaged to Bryan Guinness. Jim received the news of Diana's engagement with little enthusiasm. It came like a 'cruel blow' which greatly upset him. Diana attempted to console him with a short, but sweet, letter: 'I know you will like him [Bryan] because he is too angelic and not rough and loathes shooting and loves travelling and all the things I love.' She was preoccupied with a glamorous, materialistic world, and given Bryan's wealth, it served to make Jim feel worthless. 'When we are married and live in London, you must often come and see us,' she gently coaxed him. He sent Diana a wedding present of books, and apart from her customary thank you note, he did not set eyes on her for the next 25 years.

Quotations from the letters between Diana Mitford and James Lees-Milne were taken from *James Lees-Milne: The Life* by Michael Bloch (John Murray, 2009) and reprinted with permission in *Mrs Guinness: The Rise and Fall of Diana Mitford* (The History Press, 2015).

FINDING EDITH OLIVIER

Words by Anna Thomasson

The Reverend Dacres Olivier, rector of Wilton and private chaplain to the Earl of Pembroke, was a force to be reckoned with. Born on the last day of 1872, Edith, the eighth of his ten children, was a clever, imaginative girl who longed to run away to sea or to take to the stage; a career resolutely forbidden by her father. Throughout her life Edith had supernatural visions and claimed to feel the elemental energies of her beloved Wiltshire in her bones. But above all she was a dutiful daughter and would dedicate much of her life to her controlling father. At the age of 12, Edith began to write a diary and for the rest of her life it became an escape, and a subtle act of rebellion.

Though her brothers left for school, Edith and her sisters remained at home. She would study history at Oxford for some terms in the early 1890s, there befriending Lewis Carroll with whom she enjoyed tête-à-tête dinners in his rooms. But after that she returned to the rectory, to sit on local committees and to care for her father with her younger sister, Mildred. There, it seemed, Edith would remain. Later, during the First World War she established the Women's Land Army and was given an MBE for her work.

Edith and Mildred made a pact that they would never leave each other. And when their father died in 1919, the sisters were finally free to live their own lives. The Earl of Pembroke offered them the Daye House, a fairy-tale cottage tucked away behind a high stone wall in woods that had inspired Sidney's *Arcadia*. And so their lives could have continued, entertaining their nephews and nieces, Mildred at her piano and Edith devouring the books that she read at a speed of three a week. But then Mildred was diagnosed with breast cancer and died in November 1924.

Sitting in bed one night, Edith wrote in her diary: 'I feel very weary . . . I cannot realize that I am going to be lonely always.' It seemed her story had come to an end. But in the new year an invitation arrived from her young friend Stephen Tennant, summoning her to a villa on the Italian Riviera.

Stephen was the son of Edith's great friend, Pamela Grey. He was 18 and a student at the Slade School of Art. Aristocratic, mercurial and golden-haired, Stephen was obsessed by his own loveliness and by the loveliness of things around him. As a boy, when his father asked him what he wanted to be when he grew up, Stephen answered: 'I want to be a great beauty, sir.' At the Slade he had found a kindred spirit.

Rex Whistler was from a different world. Born in 1905, he was a builder's son from Eltham. He had an extraordinary talent for drawing and was happier sketching from his imagination than from reality. He had left school, which he hated, at the age of 16, having spent most of his time doodling in the margins of his exercise books, and gone to art school in London. Soon he was the star pupil at the Slade.

Stephen swept Rex into a rarefied world of luxury and beauty and exquisite houses in the country. But Rex was rather different to Stephen. He always remained on the fringes of high society. He was diffident, enigmatic, a romantic figure. His art, which was to make him famous, was more inspired by the romance of the past than by the avant garde of the 1920s. He is often likened to Charles Ryder in *Brideshead Revisited*, Evelyn Waugh's lament for a lost world of country house splendour. Stephen had tuberculosis and had been advised by his doctors to leave his home for warmer climes. This he planned to do, taking his new friend with him. They departed in October, after their trip had been announced in the social column of the *Daily Mirror*.

Rex dreaded the arrival of a 50-something-year-old spinster. And so he was delighted by the loquacious little woman before him, drawing on a cigarette, animatedly kicking out her foot and debating with them all about the love of power at dinner that first night. It was clear that Edith was no ordinary bluestocking. Soon the boys were giving her a makeover: a bingle haircut (cropped and shingled), lipstick and shorter dresses bought in Nice and Monaco. 'I am afraid I am rather absurdly old to do it but it does suit me,' she wrote in her diary. But perhaps most significantly, despite an age difference of over 30 years (Edith was 52 and Rex 19) it soon became clear that they were going to be great friends. The friendship was to be the most important of their lives.

The joy of writing biography is in seeking out the traces of a life. My research had initially focussed on Rex but as I began to discover him someone else came sharply into view. Edith sprang from the footnotes of biographies, from the edge of other lives, much older than Rex and his friends, but often at the centre of their photographs, holding court with a cigarette in her hand. In Wiltshire, I spent happy weeks poring over Edith's diaries. And as I read them, this fascinating woman moved from the fringes to the centre of the story. The narrative of her life, and her friendship with Rex, came tumbling out of the many volumes of her diary and her boxes of letters. As I explored her archive the traces of her life, year by year, began to emerge from the pages.

Edith was profoundly sensitive to the spirit of place and it seemed only right that I should go in search of her and indulge in what Antonia Fraser describes as optical research – namely, sightseeing. In Wilton I loitered outside the gates of the rectory where Edith had spent her childhood and was invited in by its kindly owner to see for myself the graceful hall, the warren of attics and the wide lawn that sweeps down to the river and borders the Wilton estate. I was intrigued to see the extravagant Italianate church where Dacres Olivier was rector and beside it the neat, Georgian rectory where he lived with his family. The contrast is strangely English and strangely harmonious. It struck me that there was a likeness to Edith herself, with all her jostling contradictions, here too, the conservative and the flamboyant sat happily together.

The magic of Wilton allowed Rex to escape from a childhood blighted by the death of his elder brother and by his unhappiness at school, not to mention the expectations of his dearly loved mother. On sightseeing expeditions Edith took Rex to all the places that she loved. And she introduced him to society. They became absorbed into each other's worlds. When Rex was offered his first major commission at the Tate Gallery and as his star began to rise on the London art scene, it was to the Daye House that he fled, for the counsel and companionship of his new friend. At the very heart of their friendship was a profoundly romantic sensibility which they shared.

Soon Edith was wearing Charles James couture, going to nightclubs and drinking cocktails with the Ballets Russes at the Savoy. She was going to house parties in maisonettes, where she observed 'dazed drunken faces slowly rotating in a room'. She became a successful novelist, she wrote journalism and made radio broadcasts. All the while maintaining her faith and her devotion to Wiltshire.

The Bright Young People emerged in the years after the end of the First World War. Their scandalous antics shocked society, while the press fanned the flames, and it was all to be captured in the novels of Evelyn Waugh and Nancy Mitford. Party-going, gender-bending, cocktail-drinking sybarites – they were determined to rebel against the warmongering sins of their Edwardian fathers and dance in fancy dress until dawn. Holidaying with Stephen in the south of France, Edith and Rex met the young photographer Cecil Beaton, who Stephen, by then hailed as the brightest of the bright young things, had been itching to meet.

Edith's literary career was blossoming and her world was opening up. Her portrait, taken by Beaton, appeared in *Vogue* alongside other contemporary writers. She had become an honorary bright young thing. She was free, as her friends were. She was wise, inspiring, a catalyst to their creativity and open-minded about their homosexuality at a time when it was illegal. Her novels are filled with old people who are fearful of change. They disapprove of the young and their antics. They dislike modernity and fear innovation. Edith quite consciously saw herself as the opposite of all this. She revelled in the young.

The Daye House became a retreat, not just for Rex, but for all the younger friends that were gradually forming a circle around her. Stephen Tennant and his lover, the poet Siegfried Sassoon; Brian Howard; William Walton, who spent several months at the Daye House, bringing with him a piano on which to compose his first symphony; and Cecil Beaton, for whom Edith was 'all the muses'.

I became fascinated by Edith's close circle of younger male friends, and the way their lives gradually interwove with Edith's own in the course of her diaries and letters. As I opened the envelopes, looked at their choices of paper and ink, and their handwriting, those friends came alive for me too: Stephen Tennant, self-obsessed and amusing, his loopy handwriting in pink ink on pink paper; Siegfried Sassoon, affectionate, neat, controlled; and Cecil Beaton, entertaining and ostentatious, his headed notepaper sent from grand houses and hotels in Hollywood.

In Edith's scrapbooks, which her great-great niece showed me later in my research, I found invitations to first nights, dinner menus and poems handwritten by the famous poets she knew. There were photographs by Beaton of Edith and their friends. There were prayers, postcards, quotations from essays and charms against poison. There were Rex's drawings on scraps of paper and newspaper cuttings.

In her archive there were Rex's letters, still lovingly preserved by the families that inherited them. Less because of what he wrote and more for the charming illustrations that coil around the paper and the envelope. And so, I saw Edith from another perspective and in turn I began to unravel Rex's seemingly charmed, but in fact rather troubled and ultimately tragic life.

Edith always straddled two worlds. Though so much had changed she was still in many ways the same woman she had always been. In the month that she appeared in *Vogue*, Edith was busy compiling a selection of country recipes and cures for a Women's Institute book. One day Edith might be entertaining poets or dining with politicians in London, the next she would find herself back in her old world. More pressing than a commission from *Vogue* (which she longed for) was the need for a new set of false teeth and preparing embroidery lessons for the Wilton W.I. She threw herself into local politics, later becoming the first female mayor in Wilton's history. When the Second World War came it was a call to arms for both Edith and Rex. But it would divide them forever.

Later, when Edith died, though she had never let anyone read them during her lifetime, she left the many volumes of her diary, in the hope, I believe, that they would one day shed light not only on her beloved Rex's life, but also, perhaps more importantly, on her own. 'Darling Edith,' Stephen would later write to Cecil, beside a sketch he had drawn of her: a vital little woman, a pen in her hand and stars at her feet. 'Her genius for loving her friends set her apart,' he wrote. 'She was a practitioner of the loving spirit – She made of friendship a fine art – a miracle.'

But this was all in the future, a future that Edith could never have guessed at, when she received Stephen Tennant's invitation to San Remo in early 1925. There I'd like to leave you, with Edith sailing for France en route to Italy. On board the boat she had begun a new volume of her diary. And it was the last day of winter.

❧ Anna Thomasson was born in 1980 in Staffordshire. After flirting with fashion and a stint in Paris, she studied for an MPhil in Biography under the exacting eye and inspiring guidance of historian and biographer Jane Ridley. Her thesis was shortlisted for the *Daily Mail* Biographers' Club Prize, and this formed the backbone of her debut book, *A Curious Friendship*.

LADY BLANCHE HOZIER

Words by Sonia Purnell

When I visited Lord Stanley of Alderley to research my book on Clementine Churchill, it was fun to look through his extensive album of family photographs. Almost everyone of the past few generations of this illustrious family was present; but there was one noticeable gap. Above the hand-written name of Lady Blanche Hozier, the space for the photograph was empty, although no-one seemed to know why.

Perhaps it had something to do with the fact that Lady Blanche – with her beautiful blonde hair and seraphic face – was widely considered within the family of her time to be 'mad'. She had, after all, broken so many of the rigid Victorian conventions that had defined her early life and overshadowed even her later years. Her natural rebelliousness may have made her a popular 'aunt Natty' to the young Mitford sisters (who were awestruck by her elegant defiance), but it barred her from many a smart London salon and even many of her own family gatherings.

She was born the eldest daughter of the 10th Earl of Airlie and grew up in a romantically haunted castle in the Scottish Highlands. It was Lady Blanche's mother (also known as Blanche) who was a member of the Stanley tribe of assertive and erudite English matriarchs, and who was the dominant force in the household.

The Stanleys' radical Liberal views did not exactly chime, however, with Lady Blanche's unconventional approach to such issues as marital fidelity (of which she was not in favour), extravagant spending (which she adored) or the need for female education (deemed only partly necessary).

A sort of Victorian wild-child who threatened to become a major embarrassment, Lady Blanche was hastily married off by her parents at the age of 25 to Colonel Henry Hozier. Alas, Henry had neither the fortune she was hoping for nor much in the way of warm feelings towards her. Serially unfaithful, he declared he was not interested in having children and left Lady Blanche largely to her own devices while he pursued a slightly rackety career at Lloyd's of

London.

Bored, sexy and lonely she soon sought comfort – and the prospect of children – in the arms of other men. One of her most attentive lovers, it would seem, was the 1st Baron Redesdale, Bertie Mitford, and later to become, of course, the grandfather of the Mitford sisters. He was handsome, kind and in possession of those dazzling Mitford eyes. He was also married to Lady Blanche's sister Lady Clementine, with whom he already had several children.

We should perhaps pay tribute to Lady Clementine for sharing her husband in this way with her sister. For he is almost certainly the father of at least Lady Blanche's first two children. Lady Blanche liked to circulate conflicting rumours on the paternity of her brood – perhaps in part to protect the reputation and pride of her own sister. But it is noticeable how her second daughter – born in haste on the drawing room floor in 1885 – also had dazzling sapphire-blue eyes and a similar profile to Bertie's. Named Clementine – perhaps in honour of the forbearance of her aunt – she went on to marry Winston Churchill. No doubt he came to realise that Bertie was probably not only the young Clementine's uncle by marriage, but her father too. After all, it was Bertie who was sitting next to Lady Blanche in the front row at Winston and Clementine's wedding. Clementine junior was therefore probably related to Nancy, Pamela, Unity, Jessica and Diana Mitford in more ways than one.

Lady Blanche went on to have four children in total – Kitty, Clementine and the twins Nellie and Bill. It is highly unlikely that any was Hozier's, as he himself quickly realised. Lady Blanche's frantic love-life was spectacularly well-known, complete with lurid tales of fights between jealous rivals. The numbers were equally astonishing, as she was widely reputed to keep up to ten lovers on the go at once. Her unstuffy attitude to life was clearly quite a draw, and even at her worst moments she was inevitably stylishly if unconventionally dressed.

Divorce soon followed – as did exclusion from the sort of upper-class circles in which she would normally have been expected to move. It was not so much the bed-hopping that counted against her, as the brazen way in which she conducted it. Respectable upper-class ladies of the time made sure they provided their husband with an heir, before discreetly taking on one lover at a time. Lady Blanche did neither.

Hozier, a cold and splenetic man now with a sense of grievance, refused to pay alimony and Lady Blanche was reduced to living on family handouts and the odd bit of cash from writing cookery articles for the press. She was quickly reduced to moving from one set of cheap lodgings to another to stay one step ahead of her creditors. And yet despite this itinerant life with her brood, she made each temporary home a haven of simple, good taste – complete with billowing white curtains and spotless white sofas – all on a budget. Her food was also famously good – even if sometimes she was too distracted or even hard-up to put it on the table for her own children.

She nevertheless still evidently feared the retribution of her ex-husband, and was concerned that Henry might try to take one of her children to live with him. To this effect, she once packed up overnight in their rooms in the Channel town of Seaford and fled to France with her children the very next morning. Lady Blanche settled her young family in Dieppe, where she proceeded to lose what money she had at the casino and forced her elder daughters to ask for credit to buy food in the shops. She also took up with the artist Walter Sickert – recently implausibly named as the possible real identity of Jack the Ripper. Sickert, an ill-tempered man, was also carrying on with a Mme Villain, the queen of the Dieppe fishmarket and mother of several children looking uncannily like Sickert. To her children's horror, Lady Blanche would engage in jealous exchanges with Mme Villain in the street. These altercations – and her insistence on wearing her hair in a plait down her back rather than in the traditional bun – were mystifying for the local French who expected something rather different from a titled English milady.

This sojourn in France came to an abrupt end around a year after the death of Lady Blanche's favourite and eldest daughter, Kitty. Lady Blanche never even tried to disguise her feelings for this puckish and pretty girl over the then shy and more nervous Clementine. Kitty even advised her younger sibling to try to ignore her mother's hurtful neglect as 'she can't help it'. Kitty developed typhus, probably from drinking contaminated water, and died just short of her 17th birthday. Lady Blanche never recovered from the tragedy, and merely withdrew further from Clementine, whom she deemed too judgmental and reserved for her tastes.

The family returned to England, where Lady Blanche set up home in Berkhamsted, just outside London, to take advantage of the local schools. She was intent on launching Clementine into the sort of smart society from which she was now excluded and thought her daughter needed more polish. That also meant, in Lady Blanche's view, making sure that her daughter did not destroy her marriage prospects by learning such unladylike subjects as maths. She believed young women should be intelligent and educated, but only in languages such as French and German and other appropriate humanities subjects rather than 'unseemly' sums.

Over time, Lady Blanche became more irascible and dictatorial; disappointment in her own life only added to her increasingly tetchy demeanour. Even when Clementine was a young woman, her mother would think nothing of boxing her ears when displeased and seemed to have little affection for her daughter – although she was very much in favour of her new husband, Winton Churchill. Lady Blanche's increasing drinking only served to widen the distance between the two women – and to cause concern with the younger Nellie and Bill. Lady Blanche eventually went back to settle in Dieppe once more, throwing away what money she had in the casino there. She may well have made the move precisely because casinos were still illegal in Britain.

It was there that she died, lonely and impoverished, in March 1925. Clementine was by her side as she endured her final illness, but they were never entirely reconciled. Clementine felt her childhood had been largely loveless and had left her with profound insecurities. Churchill, however, had a higher regard for a woman whose pride, tenacity and sense of style had never faltered. On the occasion of Lady Blanche's death, he wrote that he was 'glad & proud to think her blood flows in the veins of our children'.

Sonia Purnell is the author of *First Lady: The Life and Wars of Clementine Churchill* (Aurum Press). She is an author, journalist and broadcaster known for her investigative skills and lively writing style. She also writes for a variety of newspapers and is a regular broadcaster in Britain and abroad. She lives in London with her husband and two sons.

MEMORIES OF DEBO

Words by Barbara Leaming

If you are very, very lucky, someone comes into your life out of nowhere and changes everything. Debo Devonshire did that for me. I certainly didn't deserve her – no one could deserve someone quite that wonderful. Actually it was Andrew Devonshire who first invited me to Chatsworth and it was Andrew who gave me the first incredible gifts I was to receive – and the greatest of those gifts was Debo. I shall always remember Debo that first night: that night she was performing for Andrew as well as for me. 60 years into their marriage, Andrew was a rapt audience. It was not difficult to see why – though to me, during that first dinner at least, Debo was very scary. That night, it was Andrew who was the gentle one, Debo the one with whom I was sure I could never dare relax. But it changed – not least because that first night I realised that one of Debo's greatest qualities was that she was interested in everything, really everything. She wanted details; she wanted to know how things worked; she wanted to know EXACTLY what you meant when you said something—and not an iota of that interest was faked. And she would ask questions that no one else would dare to ask. Alone together upstairs in her sitting room late that first night, she made me pull up my trouser leg to see if I had the 'great legs all American girls have'. I didn't, but I did pull up the trousers – actually SHE pulled up the trouser leg. It was an extraordinary night – not least because I fell in love with both Andrew and Debo that night – and completely unexpectedly the seeds of a friendship were planted.

I'm so glad that I had the luck to see Debo with Andrew for no matter how much I was later to hear about the two of them from Debo herself and also from their family and friends, I would not have understood the complexity of that relationship had I not actually watched him watch her and her watch him.

I was in England then to research my biography of President John F. Kennedy. My husband and I had a flat on Eaton Place not far from Debo's Chatsworth Shop on Elizabeth Street. The little shop was a very special place – pure Debo – and she loved it and was deeply involved with it. My husband used to buy all of his lunches there and I still giggle thinking about how I would come home to find David on the phone with Debo in intense discussion of the merits of her soups and especially detailed reports about the prices of an item she was selling versus the price of a similar item in a supermarket on the King's Road. When the Chatsworth Shop closed later, I had an urgent phone call from her cousin Jean, warning me that Debo was so upset that I must be careful not even to mention the closing for a time.

After Andrew died, by which time Debo and I had become friends – initially, I believe, because Andrew made sure it happened – and by which time we had other deep friendships in common, Debo did not draw back, but rather expanded the wings of her friendship.

She and Andrew had been indispensable to my research for my biography of President John F. Kennedy and to my understanding of the man and the world in which JFK lived. But for the book I wrote next, about Winston Churchill, Debo, now alone, went much further. First she listened to what I hoped to do with Churchill – and then she took charge. Debo never had to be asked to help. She just offered – no rather, she ACTED. Before I knew it, she had made up lists of people I must talk to about Churchill, including her cousin Mary Soames – and then moved on to make sure they talked to me – and then made sure that I asked the right questions. She wrote letters; she made calls; she went over ideas with me. It was endless and she was incredible.

Debo loved to give advice – especially about how to do things cheaply. I still laugh thinking about her voice on the phone the day I moved into the flat I'd rented in Mayfair to do Churchill research. Our flat was not far from the Beau Brummell house she still owned, and she was full of detailed instructions about where to go in Shepherd Market – but better, still, about what to do cheaply. Debo loved the idea of doing things cheaply. 'Keep your hands in your pockets!' as she put it.

When I went up to stay with Debo at Edensor, it was strange at first to think that Andrew was gone – or rather, that he was next door, as she reminded me – in St Peter's churchyard. But she was so funny, so over the top about everything as usual. So welcoming. There was, I think, more emotion now that Andrew was gone – more sense of time passing. And always, more reminders not to waste a minute – to grab everything you can, while you can.

I can still hear her as we sat on the old-fashioned swing on the lawn in front of the vicarage talking about Andrew; talking about 'the cousinhood'; talking about people that both of us knew – people she had somehow miraculously brought into my life – who were now gone. As she talked about all that she missed, suddenly the swing started moving faster because Debo also wanted to talk about the future. What she wanted to do next – and a reminder that I must not just be thinking about what I was doing now, but what came NEXT.

Debo and Andrew are also very much there in my new book on Jackie Kennedy [*Jacqueline Bouvier Kennedy Onassis: The Untold Story*] – all sorts of things they told me about the aftermath of the assassination – as well as about what was going on during the presidency. And I am going to return in detail to that world which they opened to me with unimaginable generosity in the book I am writing next. So much of what they shared with me has vanished now – but my mind is filled with images of that vanished world – a world that strangely enough has become part of my own future.

I can't bear to think that there will never be another letter from Debo turning up in the post, that the phone will never ring again with her voice on the other end inviting me to stay with her in Edensor, that there will be no more long talks about the members of 'The Set', and, of course, that there will be no more books from her to treasure forever.

Everything about Debo had to do with life and what's next, and for that reason it is just impossible to imagine she is not out there plotting some future project.

Barbara Leaming is a *New York Times* bestselling author. Three of her books have been *New York Times* Notable Books of the Year. Her most recent book *Jacqueline Bouvier Kennedy Onassis: The Untold Story* was published in 2015. Barbara's previous book *Churchill Defiant: Fighting On 1945-1955* received The Emery Reves Award from the International Churchill Centre. Her groundbreaking biography of America's 35th President, *Jack Kennedy: The Education of a Statesman*, was the first to detail the lifelong influence of British history and culture and especially of Winston Churchill on JFK. Barbara's articles have appeared in the *New York Times* magazine, *Vanity Fair*, the *Times* of London and other periodicals.

✀ FURTHER READING ✀

A Curious Friendship: The Story of a Bluestocking and a Bright Young Thing by Anna Thomasson

Brideshead Revisited by Evelyn Waugh

Churchill's Rebels: Esmond Romilly and Jessica Mitford by Meredith Whitford

Death of a Dishonorable Gentleman by Tessa Arlen

Death Sits Down to Dinner by Tessa Arlen

Don't Tell Alfred by Nancy Mitford

First Lady: The Life and Wars of Clementine Churchill by Sonia Purnell

Hons and Rebels by Jessica Mitford

Jacqueline Bouvier Kennedy Onassis: The Untold Story by Barbara Leaming

James Lees-Milne: The Life by Michael Bloch

Love in a Cold Climate by Nancy Mitford

Mad World: Evelyn Waugh and the Secrets of Brideshead by Paula Byrne

Maverick Mountaineer by Robert Wainwright

Merton & Waugh: A Monk, A Crusty Old Man, and the Seven Story Mountain by Mary Frances Coady

Mrs Guinness: The Rise and Fall of Diana Mitford by Lyndsy Spence

Nancy Mitford by Selina Hastings

Pilgrimage by Dorothy Richardson

Television: Rare and Well Done by Terence Towles Canote

The Blessing by Nancy Mitford

The Civilian Bomb Disposing Earl: Jack Howard and Civilian Bomb Disposal in WW2 by Kerin Freeman

The Lodger by Louisa Treger

The Looking Glass House by Vanessa Tait

The Mitford Society Vol. I

The Mitford Society Vol. II

The Pursuit of Love by Nancy Mitford

❧ ABOUT THE AUTHOR ☙

Lyndsy Spence is the founder of The Mitford Society, an online community dedicated to the Mitford girls. She is the author of *The Mitford Girls' Guide to Life* (2013, The History Press) and *Mrs Guinness: The Rise and Fall of Diana Mitford* (2015, The History Press). Her forthcoming books *The Mistress of Mayfair: Men, Money and the Marriage of Doris Delevingne* (The History Press) and *Queen of the Silver Screen: The Life of Margaret Lockwood* (Fantom Films) will be published in late 2016. She has written features for *BBC News Magazine, Social & Personal, Vintage Life, Antrim Guardian, Jacquo, Silhouette* and *The Lady*. She is also a book reviewer for *The Lady*.

Printed in Great Britain
by Amazon